RAFTING THE ROLLING THUNDER

Journey Through the Grand Canyon

Frosty Wooldridge

authorHOUSE®

AuthorHouse™
1663 Liberty Drive
Bloomington, IN 47403
www.authorhouse.com
Phone: 1-800-839-8640

© 2010 Frosty Wooldridge. All rights reserved.

No part of this book may be reproduced, stored in a retrieval system, or transmitted by any means without the written permission of the author.

First published by AuthorHouse 8/25/2010

ISBN: 978-1-4343-0468-1 (sc)

Printed in the United States of America
Bloomington, Indiana

Dedicated to:

Gary V. Hall—Intrepid rafter, adventurer, poet, dancer and raconteur

"You can't pay a shrink for
what a day on the river
does for your spirit."

Contents

Foreword		ix
Chapter 1	When fear thrills every cell in your body	1
Chapter 2.	Dish fairies of the Grand Canyon appear	12
Chapter 3.	The roaring twenties kept us dancing on the water	27
Chapter 4.	Canyon Sally makes wild rush through white water fury	37
Chapter 5.	Fear has a funny way of changing your intestines	46
Chapter 6.	Satori while screaming at the top of your lungs	61
Chapter 7.	Across the sky as if pulled by chariots of fire	66
Chapter 8.	The emerging creative energy of the universe	75
Chapter 9.	Nothing! That's the beauty of it	79
Chapter 10.	Is it possible to get fat on nature's visions?	88
Chapter 11.	Go through our lives without noticing our lives	95
Chapter 12.	And miss the biggest orgasm of the trip?	100
Chapter 13.	Unholy, raging and terrifying stretch of water	108
Chapter 14.	Tales of Highwater Harry	120
Chapter 15.	How fast our lives sweep past	130
Chapter 16.	River friends and last Powell report	134
About the Author		137

Foreword

No amount of words can describe the emotional 'rush' you feel while rafting Class I, II, III, IV and V rapids on the Colorado River through the Grand Canyon. Beyond those moments of utter exhilaration and fear, something more sublime beckons your spirit into the canyon. Your eyes wander across 1.7 billion years of creation. One of my fellow rafters, Strat Hall said, "It may have taken God a few billion years, but God worked some magic in this canyon. It's a rare masterpiece!"

For over three decades, I rafted rivers all over the world. However, none match the awesome power, awe-inspiring beauty and spiritual contemplation afforded by the Grand Canyon. Without a doubt, this raft trip ranks with the top 20 adventures on the planet. It leaves you gasping in wonderment, thrilled with fear and inspired to dream magnificent thoughts while you gaze into a geological magnum opus.

Thank you Gary Hall for making this amazing trip possible. Without you, this book would not have been written. Thanks to Badger Hall for his wisdom and photographic talents with the cover. Thanks to Wocnis Hall for his stirring "Ballad of Highwater Harry."

Additionally, thanks goes to the courage of the first rafter down the Grand Canyon, John Wesley Powell and his men. Ultimately, we enjoyed a hint of historical camaraderie knowing what Powell experienced in his time, we lived in ours. The dangers he faced, we faced, too! His quest became our quest in the 21st century.

What inspired it in him? What has inspired it in us? I think human nature pushes us past our own front door and compels us into the unknown. Every human possesses adventure-yearning to some degree. Scary as it might be, we MUST move forward or sit back and die a spiritual death. Adventure exploration encompasses the core thrust of humanity.

The Wizard of Oz said, "You have plenty of courage, I am sure. All you need is confidence in yourself. There is no living thing that is not afraid when it faces danger. The true courage is in facing danger when you are afraid, and that kind of courage you have in plenty."

Finally, to you the reader—enjoy this amazing journey through time, water and sand. May it lift your spirits, power your imagination and thrust you into your own raft for a ride through the Grand Canyon.

Frosty Wooldridge Louisville, CO

CHAPTER 1 —When fear thrills every cell in your body

> *"There will always be one more river, not to cross, but to follow. The journey goes on forever, and we are fellow voyagers on our little living ship of stone and soil and water and vapor—on this delicate little planet circling round the sun, which human kind call Earth."*
>
> Edward Abbey

An anxious thrill surged through my body as if an avalanche threatened to bury me alive! But, in this case, a mountain of angry whitewater rumbled toward me—seething with power and deadly intensity. It possessed the force of a herd of stampeding buffalo thundering down on me.

One mistake and our raft could flip, and all of us would become pin-balls in nature's merciless game of rolling thunder.

In seconds, we dropped down the cool calm of the 'tongue' toward the rapid. But the closer we sped to the first 'roller', my eyes grew to resemble two fried eggs on a hot skillet. It towered above us ten feet high! What my eyes saw translated into excitement—which shot adrenaline throughout my body. But there I was, a rookie captain of the raft and in charge of taking us through 1.7 billion years of erosion—on the raging Colorado River in the middle of one of nature's prettiest creations: the Grand Canyon.

Moments earlier, Gary said, "Why don't you captain the boat?"

"You don't have to ask me twice," I said, jumping up to seize the oars.

I grabbed the big, heavy wooden oars on Gary's raft. Ahead, the quiet canyon grew into a loud roar as we neared Badger Rapid.

"Make sure you bring the boat in sideways in the middle of the tongue," he said. "As you head into it, be sure to turn the boat down river and stay in the middle of the rapids…watch for signs of disturbed water where the big boulders are hidden. Rocks are bad for the boat. Try to dive directly into the rollers head first…."

"Got it," I said, eagerly.

"For every rapid," Gary continued. "Stand up and see what you have to navigate. You really need to see where the tongue is located and if any laterals are coming in from the sides. The big key is to watch for big rocks that could hang us up or dump us."

"Okay," I said.

Receiving instructions and doing it proved a challenge. There's a knack to being a boatman on a wild ride down the Colorado River in the Grand Canyon. I followed Gary's mentoring. I angled the boat sideways down the tongue of Badger Rapid. It's amazing how the raft floated on quiet, still, peaceful water until we headed into the tempest. I cranked on the boney oars and spun the 16-foot raft headfirst. For a moment, the bow of the boat shot skyward like the lead car on a roller coaster. In those few seconds, Gary and his lady, Julie, crouching in front and hanging on to the ropes, watched a wall of water slam over the top of the raft and shatter like a plate glass window in the movies—all over them. Instantly, they nose-dived over the top of the wave and I shot skyward with both oars out of the water—looking like a dragon fly's wings out of control.

We plunged downward into the maw of hell. Only ten feet behind them in the back of the raft, I followed with the reluctance of a lamb being led to the shearing shed. The raft bent in front as it hit the bottom of the second roller. Shooting skyward, like the Challenger launching off the pad at Cape Canaveral, the raft bolted into the vacant blue sky above us. Water engulfed our raft in a million crystals of liquid excitement. Julie screamed with delight. Gary, ever the veteran rafter, hung on with sheer pleasure.

Water drenched us. No matter! We floated within the belly of the beast and I worked the oars to keep from tipping over. I dug the blades into the raging, boiling white water to keep the raft bow down river. We shot through several more six-foot rollers and quickly glided toward calmer waters.

"Yahoo!" I yelled. "What a rush!"

"I'd give you a—B," Gary said.

"We lived, didn't we?!" I answered.

So began one of the greatest adventures of my life—running the roiling, heart pounding waters of the Colorado River through the magic of the Grand Canyon. At no time have I been more thrilled through fear and excitement than when I sat as a passenger or commanded the raft on one of the world's greatest adventures.

Brenda, a long-time friend, called me months ahead, telling me that she had won a permit to raft the Grand Canyon. She invited me. I have rafted many rivers around the world, so I thought it wasn't THAT much of a big deal. I accompanied her on the Green and Yampa years before. My rafting experiences included Europe, Australia, New Zealand, Alaska, and South America. I told her I would get back with her. Gary called a day later, and told me to say "Yes" before she asked someone else to go. He said it was the greatest raft trip in the world. I wouldn't have too many more chances because the waiting time to obtain a permit exceeded 10 years.

"I'm going," I told Brenda on the phone.

"Great," she said. "Good to have you in our group."

Driving out to Page, Arizona creates a sense of barren nothingness in the mind.

"Who would want to live here?" I asked Gary.

"Someone who likes it hot and desolate," he said.

It's odd to imagine a town jumping out of the desert on the edge of the Colorado River. The landscape might as well have been on the moon. Red and tan soil along with sandstone rock dominated as mountains rose in the distance. The river couldn't be seen except where it backs up behind Glen Canyon Dam.

A golf course, replete with lush green fairways presented an unusual contrast as it butted up against rust-colored rolling desert sands.

We stopped at the Powell Museum inside the city. There, we saw a replica of John Wesley Powell's boat, the Emma Dean, which in 1869 carried him on the greatest river adventure known in the world at that time. Powell, a veteran Army officer, lost his right arm in the Civil War. He faced danger not only from the deadly river, but also from disease, starvation, hostile Indians, and desertion by his own men. Each day presented him with new challenges.

He wrote on July 11th, "A short distance below camp we ran a rapid, and in doing so, broke an oar, and then lost another, both belonging to the Emma Dean. We soon approached another rapid. Standing on the deck, I thought it could be run, and on we went. Coming nearer, I saw that at the foot it was a short turn to the left, where the waters piled up against the cliff. We tried to land, but discovered that, being in swift water above the fall, we couldn't reach shore, crippled as we were by the loss of two oars; so the bow of the boat was turned down stream. We shot past a big rock; a reflex wave rolled over our little boat and filled it with water. I saw that the place was dangerous and signaled to the other boats to land where they could. Another wave hit my boat and threw me into the water. I soon found that swimming was easy. When a breaker rolled over me, I closed my mouth and was carried through it. As soon as we reached quiet water, we swam to one side and turned over the boat. At last, we reached a huge pile of driftwood. Our rolls of blankets, two guns, and a barometer were in the open compartment of the boat and when it went over, these were thrown out. The guns and barometer were lost, but I managed to catch one of the blankets as it drifted down, but the other two were lost, and hereafter, we may sleep cold."

Gary and I toured the museum with great interest. Many men and women lived and died plying the tempestuous waters of that ancient river that cut through the canyon for millions of years.

"We're going to put-in at Lee's Ferry and float 225 miles to the Diamond Creek take-out right here," Gary said, pointing to the map.

"Looks good to me," I said, not really knowing what I was getting myself into.

"You're going to love the scenery," he said. "Some of the walls are a mile high and we'll be floating through 1.7 billion years of erosion. Nature creates a lot of magic in a billion years. We'll be seeing a lot of geological creativity."

After eating lunch and buying a few last minute supplies for the trip, we headed the truck and all our gear down to Lee's Ferry. We dropped down into the Grand Canyon along a deep narrow cliff face, the color of a slice of baked ham, and made our way along the river. At one point, we crossed over a bridge high above the Colorado. We drove along red clay rocks and sand. Sparse bushes grew along the route, and above us, blue sky garnished colorful tan-bronze canyon walls.

At Lee's Ferry, we reached the put-in late in the day. The rest of our five rafts, twelve-person crew busied themselves rigging their rafts on the shoreline. The Colorado River rolled past us as placid and quiet as a dog sleeping on the front porch on a hot day.

Gary introduced me to Badger, Wocnis, Strat (three brothers), Steve, Cindy and Rick (married), Brenda and Ivan (significant others), and Sally (with Strat). I already knew Gary and Julie. All were in their forties or fifties. Everyone enjoyed being veteran river runners. Most loved the outdoors and the 'primordial' aspect of wild living. Three proved five star hotel types, but they would 'endure' the lack of amenities for a short time. Several like me could live 'wild' for months at a time and revel in the visceral aspect of the wilderness. Those are my kind of people—relishing the "savage" in themselves.

Another rafter Robert Service said, "The summer—no sweeter was ever; The sunshiny woods all athrill; The grayling aleap in the river, The bighorn sheep on the hill. The strong life that never knows harness; The wilds where the caribou call; The freshness, the freedom, the farness—O God! How I'm stuck on it all."

It's interesting when I meet a group of people. At first they are faces and bodies; next, they become voices; soon, they become personalities; next comes characters with their passions, problems and dimensions; and finally, they become friends, or simply acquaintances in the grand parade of people who march through my life. They either become attracted to me and me to them or we simply share the moment and later, go about our lives.

Many years ago, I read a book about human perfection and how to accomplish it, but when the perfection manifested, humanity found itself bored with comfort. One man broke out of the 'perfect' living paradigm and crossed into the wilderness. He became a savage. Most people don't know it, but Hollywood (my friend Gary),

Wocnis, Badger, Strat, Steve, and maybe the quiet one, Ivan were like me, 'savages', who loved their moments in washing, no, DRENCHING themselves in the waters of the wilderness. We appreciated the bite of a mosquito, the zipping up of our bag as we slept under a starlit sky, and a campfire with a boiling pot of stew cooking over the coals and ready for our 'ravenous' bellies. We don't care if we're freezing to death or sweating our guts out in 120-degree heat. We came for the adventure! Yeah, we burp, fart, pee and love our lives in the woods. Because, in the woods, uncertainty thrives!

Heck, I've been face to face with grizzly bears, and, at the moment didn't know if tomorrow would be an option. I nearly froze to death at 18,000 feet in the Andes and welcomed death, but I didn't die. It's all a random deal. Still, I'd do it again.

My friend John Muir said it better, "...No healthy man who delivers himself into the hands of nature can possibly doubt the doubleness of his life. Soul and body receive separate nourishment and separate exercise, and speedily reach a stage of development where-in each is easily known apart from the other. Living artificially in town, we are sickly, and never come to know ourselves. Our torpid souls are hopelessly entangled with our torpid bodies, and not only is there a confused mingling of our own souls with our own bodies, but we hardly possess a separate existence from our neighbors."

It's when a person relinquishes his/her attachment to the known by stepping into the unknown of nature that the world opens up endless possibilities. So few take the chance! Because it's safer in the known even if it's boring and continues for years. That's why people keep the same jobs. They might heed the Buddha when he said, "Find a job you like and you won't have to work a day for the rest of your life." If a person engages life—life opens its magic, wonder, exhilaration and fullness.

Nonetheless, I always walk away learning something from everyone on such a journey. Every single person on this trip taught me a lesson whether they knew it or not. Some of the lessons proved positive and some turned out otherwise. All proved valuable. For each lesson, I am thankful the person provided it. I only hope I helped them on their life journey as they enlightened me. It all depends on whether or not they were listening, watching or interested in learning. If not, I've learned to enjoy without attachment. I've learned that everyone becomes what he or she has chosen to be.

After introductions, everyone busily prepared their rafts for the next day. Gary backed his truck down to the river. We unloaded the raft and gear. Soon, we too, spread our equipment along the shoreline like a big garage sale. We prepared the raft. We set up with a foot pump and stomped on it hundreds of times until the raft took shape. From there, we lashed the aluminum frame to the raft and began placing the cooler, drinks, 16 days of food supplies, seats, bags and straps onto the raft. Slowly, Gary's "River Slug" as he affectionately named it, took shape. The extra oars locked onto the sides of the raft. We filled the drink bag and tossed it into the 47 degree water to keep it cool. We piloted a self-contained, 16 feet long, and seven feet wide, gray with red/black trim lines—river running adventure craft. One sobering item—it wasn't a self-bailer. That meant the person in front bailed when the rapid dropped countless gallons of water inboard.

We embarked from Lee's Ferry. Prospectors and travelers crossed at that point on the river in the 1850s through to 1929. John D. Lee operated a large flat boat. Horses, Indians and cowboys crossed for mere pennies per trip. In 1912, a steamer named the Charles H. Spencer hauled coal to Lee's Ferry, but sank on the third trip. It's still sunk in the bottom of the river.

Next to us, a group of twenty-something's rigged their boats and talked loudly. Before our eyes, they unloaded 102 cases of beer.

"Are you going to drink all that beer on this trip?" I asked.

"You got that right," one of them said.

"We used to drink that much, too," Brenda said. "But our crew has high blood pressure, high cholesterol, prostate problems, weak livers and one heart attack."

"That's TOO funny!" one of the younger women shot back.

"It's not if you're the one with the heart attack," Badger said.

"Right on!" one of the twenty-something's said.

"Ah," I said. "As the writer Emerson commented, "Youth! It's wasted on the young.""

Later, we set up our tents in the tree line by the river. The ranger drove down to give us notice that he would return in the morning to present an orientation on rafting the Grand Canyon. The guy's size rivaled one of those balloon floats at a Macy's Thanksgiving Day parade.

We ate dinner at a restaurant near Lee's Ferry. It catered to river runners with pictures on the walls of white water rafts splashing through the rapids and being upended. The pictures looked wild, but still, I didn't have a clue.

Back at camp on the river, Julie arrived with Sally. Rick picked them up at the airport. Our group congealed! I walked around the ruins that had been a small town, complete with post office. Miners in the 1850s tried to ore gold from the hills, but failed. As I walked back, I read a sign from the park service, "Down the river lies heart pounding adventure."

Above me, the sky glowed with golden hues along with streamers flying across the heavens from wispy clouds skittering on their indolent journey to places around the globe. They floated on a sojourn, too, and probably just as important to them. As I stood there, watching my new friends talk and work—the last light of the sun shown like burning torches lighting up the canyon walls in burnished browns, reds and tan. Happy voices! Hands gesturing! Laughter! Great expectations! All felt good in the world— at least, our part of it.

I walked over to my tent. Once inside my bag, I sat up and took one last look at the river. A quiet, black sheet of glass spread before me. I placed my life into its hands for the next 16 days.

"Heart pounding adventure," I muttered to myself. "Works for me!"

Sleep came quickly in the wilderness. Better than a five star hotel!

CHAPTER 2—Dish fairies of the Grand Canyon appear

> *"The strong current bears us toward the overhanging wall on the outside of the river. A sure deathtrap! Wrapped on stone by a liquid hand with the force of a mountain in its pressure, we would drown like rats in a rain barrel pushed under by wanton boys with brooms. Panic, terror, suffocation—not even our life jackets could save us there. Something to think about, I think, as I contemplate the imminent danger, and meditate upon possible alternatives to a sudden, sodden, personal extinction. Walt Blackadar, world's greatest kayaker, died in similar fashion beneath a jammed half-sunken tree on the Payette River in Idaho."*
>
> Edward Abbey

A brown colored hawk glided quietly on his breakfast patrol along the cliffs in the early morning sunlight. I peeked out my tent flaps to see him flying about his business. The glint of the sun flashed off his white belly. His keen eyes intently searched for a mouse or other rodent. Up he rose into the cobalt sky, and down again, along the brown/tan canyon walls above the river. The hawk soared as poetry in motion—a perfect blend of speed and grace. It reminded me of John Muir's words: "A lifetime is so little time that we die before we get ready to live." Those words give me support that I've done the right thing by gulping down life every year of each decade of my life instead sipping at it while awaiting retirement.

The hawk soared out of sight. Time to break camp! Even in the early morning, the heat of the day descended upon us. The ranger said it had been 110 degrees everyday for most of August and into September.

Slowly, our crew gathered to drink fruit juice and eat muffins provided by Brenda. Sally, Cindy, Julie and Brenda comprised our haute cuisine for the trip. Brenda comprised the brains and culinary artistry behind all the great food we expected to eat. Sally, Julie and Cindy made for a perfect support crew.

Final preparations proceeded as to vehicle transport to take-out, and checklists of items needed by crew persons. The ranger arrived around 10:00 a.m. to check photo IDs and make sure we knew the rules of the river. We stood around in a circle as he talked about checking for scorpions, red ants and mice.

"Please be careful to check any of your gear that's been on the ground," he said. "Shake it out or you might have a scorpion sting you won't ever forget."

He covered using the 'Groover' (toilet), and safety rules.

Minutes later, we stood for a group picture beside the rafts. Everyone scattered onto his or her boat after the last, "Say cheeeeeese!"

It's a special feeling being on the front end of a great adventure. I never cease my appreciation at my own good fortune to have been able to go on so many over the years.

This raft trip down the Grand Canyon provided another 'big gulp' of life.

Julie and I pulled on our life vests and shoved the River Slug into the current. Gary sat back in the captain's seat with a REALLY big grin on his face. This was his river, his time, and his life pleasure. He rafted many rivers in North America all the way into South America.

Two green lawn chairs locked into place on the front board of the raft. You couldn't find better seats on the 50-yard line at an NFL game. Straps at all four corners secured them. On the front of the raft, several straps locked into the D-rings so we could hold on when needed. We locked everything into place. Two ammo cases strapped to the sides of the raft secured Gary and Julie's cameras, valuables and reading materials.

Sitting there chatting with Julie, I couldn't help but feel a chill of excitement because we embarked on the most stunning white water river raft trip in the world. Added to that, we floated along the same river John Wesley Powell explored 140 years earlier in 1869.

Paria Ripples provided the first rapid—nothing to talk about. The water became a gentle rapid as if water ran over a cheese grater. It turned white but no violent action. On both sides of the river, green scrub trees grew in fits and starts. They gave a nice contrast to the eternal brown/red sandstone rock that dominated the walls that rose away from the river. Further along the Colorado, many colors combined to make a swirling-like marbled ice cream. We floated through Marble Canyon. The ancient walls jutted 1,000 feet into the sky. As we floated further into the trip, they soared to heights of 5,000 feet. That seemed hard to imagine as we paddled into the first moments of the adventure.

On August 5, 1869, Powell wrote, "With some feeling of anxiety we entered a new canyon this morning. We have learned to observe closely the texture of the rock. In softer strata we have a quiet river; in harder strata we find rapids and falls. Below us are the lime stones and sand stones which we found in Cataract Canyon. This bodes toil and danger."

Julie and I sat on our lawn chairs in the front of the raft watching the other rafters in front of us. The quiet flapping of the oars on each boat gave the look of a two-legged water bug slowly moving across the surface. The amazing aspect of the river from mile zero at Lee's Ferry was that it presented an utterly peaceful countenance. Tranquil clear green waters moved over a rocky riverbed. We watched fish lazily maintaining their position in the water as they stayed behind rocks and boulders on the bottom. A blue sky wedged between massive silent rock cliffs above the river. Nothing about the scene indicated any "heart pounding adventure" or fear of the many rapids along the 225 miles of the canyon.

We swept through a series of small rapids that barely splashed any water into our rafts. After riding through each rapid, the river settled back into its quiet journey through the canyon. We, too, 'settled' back into our rafts.

With each passing mile, the canyon walls rose higher into the sky. We floated the sleepy waters of the river, but tan/yellow/red rock cliffs and a narrow blue sky dominated our world. Essentially, we traveled through ancient sand dunes that had been compacted into layered rock. With millions of years of being laid down, it provided unending visual interest in the way it was being torn down via erosion. To place our route in perspective, we traveled 225 miles downriver through 1.7 billion years of erosion. I could only imagine what kind of magic nature had worked in such a great expanse of time.

Overhead, canyon walls presented endless cracks, fissures, layers and blocks of rock formations. Avalanche chutes of rock broke away from some walls and crashed into the river. At some junctures, dry waterfalls waited for the next rain so they could return to action.

Closer to the river, an endless procession of scrub trees and bushes painted the shoreline in shades of green.

Julie sat reading her book and asked us questions about what "lies" were acceptable. She gave quite a few scenarios on what kind of lies should be told at different times. She made Gary and me think in a place where we didn't want to think. But, after thinking about it, we started thinking.

From there, we got into quality of life issues, living and dying. I found it interesting that many women look at life differently than males. Seems they think it's good to live even with legs amputated or arms missing. "Oh, you could do a lot of things if you were blind, or had two legs amputated…there's still much you could do with your life."

At some point, if the quality or degree of living is unacceptable to a person, they may decide to take themselves out. For instance, I would not live like the late Christopher Reeve in a wheel chair, on a ventilator driven by an electric motor for my every breath, and totally paralyzed except for my mouth and eye lids. Since he chose to live like that, he made his decision. I'd kill myself or demand to let my death happen, immediately. I'd pull my own plug if I could.

Yes, I respect his decision and I respect my decision. What would you do? It's up to you. Self-euthanasia proves a respectful and a reasonable choice in my book. I sure as hell wouldn't want to hang around like Reeve did, or for that matter, Ronald Reagan with Alzheimer's Disease for the last ten years of his life. To waste away into a blithering idiot drooling on myself and doing my pants daily is not my idea of quality of living. Also, that kind of demise works untold misery on loved ones.

Hurrah for Dr. Kevorkian! As Helen Keller said, "Life is either a daring adventure, or it is nothing. Security is mostly a superstition. It does not exist in nature." Good for you, Helen. You were a gutsy lady. I respect your choices. Kick some tail feathers!

Thank you, Julie, for bringing up these thinking moments on the river. I mean, what the heck else were we to do with our time while we paddled through nature's creativity?!

As we drifted, we heard other conversations in each boat. Peacefulness dominated! Julie, a woman of incredible time constraints and schedules to meet in her normal life, asked about the time. I said, "River time." She looked at me with a skewered face. "What?"

"You know," I said. "It's river time…I mean, no time… anytime…sometime. What I mean is time doesn't matter while we're on the river. Do you have any place you have to be this morning? This afternoon? It's just here and now…nothing more and nothing less. For that matter it's either day time or night time. Do you have any classes you have to teach?"

"No," she said. "I just wanted to know what time it was."

"For what?" I asked. "What will you do with knowing the time?"

She smiled. I saw a certain relaxation beam over her face. And, as I noticed in the following days, she moved into 'river time' with a delightful freeing of her soul. 'River time' agreed with Julie. Gary hit it the moment he dug the oars into the water. He taught it to me. Thanks, Gary.

Along the way, an overhang of black rock reflected rippling waters. It was yet another natural marvel to place in my "memory box of wonders" I had seen in the world.

At Soap Rapid, I eased the boat into a wild, raging, green water cataract. Six-foot rollers (waves) lined up to dunk us into the drink. But I followed Gary's instructions and brought the raft into position sideways into the middle of the main flow called the 'tongue'. Like a funnel, the tongue delivers the raft and all passengers into the middle of raging white water rollers.

I nosed the big raft dead center into the watery tempest. For a moment, all remained still. I saw huge white waves ahead. Gary and Julie braced for the ride.

Instantly, the boat dropped like the nose of a roller coaster into the "hole." Just as quickly, the nose of the raft shot skyward like a rocket being launched. The raft bent like a pretzel in the front section.

By the time it hit the top of the eight-foot wall of water, it quickly dove over the top and plunged downward—but this time a wall of water crashed in from the side. At that moment, the white, boiling river slammed into Julie and Gary—soaking them and filled the bottom of the raft.

I kept pressure on the oars to keep the boat heading straight into the next wave, which I did, but as the raft moved out of the next roller, I pulled hard on the oar—only to have it rip out of the oar lock.

Gary saw my dilemma and helped me place the oar back into the slot. The boat had spun sideways, but by that time, the waves diminished to three feet allowing the raft to move into the roiling waters outside the main flow. We spun around like a "tea cup" ride at the carnival.

"YAHOO!" Julie yelled with delight.

An oarsman commands the craft. Once into the tempest of the rapids, anything can happen, good or not so good. I might maintain control one moment and totally race out of control the next. We might be floating over the 'wildness' one moment and seconds later, we could be swimming for our lives. Precarious feelings rushed through my body. I liked it, yet I respected my circumstances.

For certain, riding the rapids provided a heart pounding adrenaline rush. As in a football game with 15 seconds left on the clock with first and goal—anything can happen. We made it through the rest of the day without incident until we reached House Rock Rapid.

"I'll take us through," Gary said.

As we neared the rapid, Gary and I stood up on the raft to scout the location of the tongue. From where we were, we could hear the roar of the water, but the drop was so deep, we could not see the rapids themselves. Within moments, however, House Rock commanded our attention. It roared like a thousand angry, caged lions. The tongue of the main flow shot down a long runway off to the left side of the river.

At the end of it, a big, ugly, scary series of waves—that resembled a giant wheat combine on the farms in Kansas—waited to gobble us up. The aspirin white water seethed with ominous rage.

Julie and I crouched just behind the air chamber on the front of the raft. I glanced back at Gary. He possessed the look of a veteran boatman who respected the river and maintained a quiet confidence with his ability to take the boat through the furious white water ahead.

Being face to face with the rapids presented a whole new perspective. Julie and I were the lead characters in a carnival bumper-car rally gone out of control. This time, the tongue swept us smoothly into the first roller, which swept upward toward the sky. On our left, a fang of rock threatened to rip through our rubber boat. One moment I saw blue and the next, liquid green. Just as quickly, a wall of white took a Mohammed Ali round house punch to our faces. A glance at Julie showed a face surprised at how big and how nasty the 'thing' in front of us had grown.

We hung on for dear life. An eight-foot wall of white wrath smashed into us. We rafted into a Hurricane Katrina tidal wave. It slapped our bodies back as we hung on to the front straps. We ran into six more huge walls of water that repeatedly crashed into our raft. We rode the meanest "Fu-man-chu" bull at a rodeo.

"Need some bailers," Gary said.

"No kidding," I said, as I grabbed the buckets for Julie and me.

We took-on 20 gallons of water in seconds. We bailed like a couple of sailors trying to save our boat from sinking.

After bailing, we settled back into our lawn chairs. The energy in my body calmed down. But the excitement echoed inside me. I looked around to see the other rafts in various positions on the river. Sometimes, we bumped into Strat and Sally, or we might match river speed with Rick and Wocnis. Badger and Steve always told good jokes. Ivan carried Cindy and Brenda in his boat. I'm sure he would know everything about women after 16 days on the river. Good energy! Rick, the comic on the trip, could turn a phrase that made us laugh out loud. At one point, I asked him what he did for a living. "I'm a lawyer," he said. I added, "Oh, you're one of those guys who steals from the rich and the poor...then call it practicing 'good law' to bring about justice, and spend the money on yourself."

"Guilty," he said, with a grin.

He took it in good stead, so no harm done. His wife, Cindy, also a lawyer wore a T-shirt that read, "Talk is cheap until you need a lawyer." No wonder there are so many lawyer jokes. I have to admit that I still can't understand why they make $350.00 an hour off all the people who make only $15.00 an hour and call it 'justice'. All they do is shuffle papers and talk to the jury. They don't actually do any 'work' that produces anything of value for our country. I mean, a truck driver transports the goods to the store and a teacher educates children and a dentist fixes teeth and a builder builds homes.

They produce something of merit. Lawyers only litigate questions of opinion. But, as with all things in life, it's just the way it is. Sooner or later, we all get into lawyers' clutches and they drive BMWs because of our troubles. I don't judge them one way or the other. It's one of the terrible inequities of life.

We drifted down stream until we camped on a sandbar nestled against the canyon wall. Everyone threw their gear onto the sand and plodded uphill until they found a suitable spot. Gary set the 'Groover' at a quiet and private location overlooking the river. Anyone that needed to do their business could take care of it in fantastic surroundings.

The males did the manly thing and pitched tents. Air mattresses inflated and sleeping bags rolled out. Everyone owned a lawn chair and circled around the 'dining room under the stars'.

The ladies set up the kitchen. Two long tables supported on metal legs held two propane stoves, cooking pots, and various tools needed for food preparation. They placed fresh water on the tables for cooking and each night cooked a separate recipe for dinner. A master chef, Brenda began preparing dinner immediately. Cindy, Julie and Sally stepped in to help. The four of them whipped up one heck of a good feed each night.

With the sun ebbing in the sky, Strat pulled out his guitar and Wocnis grabbed his harmonica. They started strumming and singing. Above us, stars began their night vigil across the narrow band of sky sandwiched between canyon walls. It grew to more than 2,000 feet over our heads.

We ate dinner. Immediately afterwards, Brenda tagged Rick, Steve and me to be the dishwashers. "Men don't do dishes," Steve said as he puffed out his chest.

Brenda, the trip leader, and no woman to ever question, walked up to him, "Pretend you're a fairy then and do a good turn by doing the dishes, because you're going to be washing dishes for the whole trip."

"Does that mean I'm a dish fairy?" Steve asked.

"Yeah," she said, commandingly. "You're all a bunch of dish fairies."

And so it came to pass, the dish fairies of the Grand Canyon, like the bats that darted about the river each night when the sun went down, appeared in the darkness after dinner ended, and began their arduous task of washing dishes.

"If I've got to be a dish fairy," I said. "Where are my wings?"

"Here," Sally said. "Try this dish towel on for your feathers."

I caught the dishtowel in mid flight. "Gee, thanks," I said, dejectedly.

"Do we have to?" Rick whined.

"If you ever want any excitement in your life again," his wife Cindy said, "you'd better get those dishes washed."

"Yes, dear…."

All the men hoped Rick would show his macho side and take command of the moment—but like the timid, wretched, mouse of a man he was, Rick shuffled his stubby, little feet, and whimpered all the way over to the plastic dish tub on the table. All three of us looked at each other, as pathetically as we could look, but sympathy did not arrive. Everyone had a job, and we got nailed with the worst one in the whole camp.

We pulled three tubs full of water from the river. After heating one tub of water for the wash, we had a middle tub for the primary rinse and placed bleach in the final rinse tub. With biodegradable soap, we washed the dishes, let them rinse for 60 seconds and then set them on the table to dry.

Each of us washed, rinsed or dried dishes. As a group, each night, we became more provocative with our comments and creative dishwashing talents. Our mantra, "NO FEAR...DISH FAIRIES FOREVER!" Once we completed washing and drying, we sifted solid foods out with a wire mesh and placed all organic waste in the trash bags for safe keeping. The rule on the river: "LEAVE NO TRACE!"

After drying, we placed all dishes and cookware into the mess box. Our job completed, we high fived each other and settled into the circle for singing songs or talking with one another.

That night, I wasn't in much of a mood for talking. I suffered wrinkled, dish pan hands along with cracked cuticles and a broken nail. I could not find a manicurist THAT far away from civilization. My wings, being dishtowels, were too wet from drying dishes, to even attempt flying. I felt trapped.

Nursing my pained male ego, I sat down by the river and pulled out my John Wesley Powell book. He had sat down after a successful day of running the rapids and pitched camp on a sandbar nearly the same place where we had pitched camp. He wrote, "This morning we had an exhilarating ride. The river was swift, and there were many smooth rapids. I stood on deck, keeping a careful watch ahead, and we glided along, mile after mile, plying strokes, now on the right and then on the left, just sufficient to guide our boats past the rocks into smooth water. At noon we emerged from a canyon and camped for dinner under a cottonwood tree standing on the left bank.

"Extensive sand plains extend back from the immediate river valley as far as we can see on either side. These naked, drifting sands gleam brilliantly in the midday sun. The reflected heat from the glaring surface produces a curious motion of the atmosphere; little currents were generated and seemed to tremble and move about in many directions, or, failing to see that the movement was in the atmosphere, it gave the impression of unstable land. Plains and hills and cliffs and distant mountains seemed to be floating vaguely about in a trembling, wave-rocked sea, and patches of landscape seemed to float away and be lost, and then, reappeared.

"Just opposite, there are buttes, outliers of cliffs to the left. Below, they are composed of shales and marls of light blue and slate colors; above, the rocks are buff and gray, and then brown. The buttes are buttressed below, where the azure rocks are seen, and terraced above through the gray and brown beds of rock. A long line of cliffs separates the tablelands through which Gray Canyon is cut. The eye can trace these beds and cliffs on either side of the river. These many cliffs are miles in length and hundreds of feet high; and all these buttes, great mountain masses of rock—are dancing and fading away and reappearing; softly moving about—or so they seem to the eye as seen through the shifting atmosphere."

Mr. Powell possessed a geologist's mind. He described hard data and did it well.

Above me that night, I saw a ragged amoeba-shaped slit—bordered by high canyon cliffs—filled with the ink black of space speckled with twinkling stars. The canyon walls above me resembled a Rorschach Blot. They imposed, but did not threaten. The river quietly curled past making no sound, but I 'felt' it moving. The sand between my toes warmed me with escaping heat from the day's 95-degree temperatures. Out on the river, dozens of bats that looked like gray, furry mice with wings, darted back and forth on their dinner patrols. Sitting by the water prompted serenity in my spirit. I'll bet Powell felt the romance of his moment just as I felt the 'spirit' of mine in my own time.

Chapter 3—The roaring twenties kept us dancing on the water

> *"A man, whose emotions are alive, is at home anywhere."*
> Saul Bellow

The day started out calmly enough. We broke camp and hit the river as the sun crept up the canyon walls.

I thought about camp last night and how everyone meshed into the flow of the river. The "Dish Fairies" had succeeded in washing all the dishes without hurting themselves. A few mice attacked some trail mix in unprotected plastic bags. In the morning, a half dozen ravens dropped out of the sky and grabbed any piece of food in sight.

The 'Groover' had been set up in a nice place on the river with a view both up and down the canyon. I have never enjoyed a more tranquil moment of repose in nature's paradise. I asked Gary why he called the shitter a 'Groover'.

"On one of our trips," he said. "We forgot the toilet seat that we place over the ammo can. Everyone who used it for their morning constitutional got a long groove down the back of his or her butt and legs. Thus, it became the 'Groover'."

"Makes sense to me," I said.

Not far into the river, the first set of rapids reared its frothing, furious head. The 21-mile rapids started what is known on the river as "The Roaring Twenties." Every fifteen to thirty minutes, we found ourselves embroiled in raging white water. No time to rest or relax! The river dropped us into its wildness at every bend in the canyon.

At one point, Badger and Steve headed into the rapids and rode high on a wave. Over half of their raft-belly shot into the air as they hung on the edge of disaster. Steve sat on the front of the raft hanging on for dear life when his legs shot skyward like two 'chicken wishbones' and Badger's yellow oars flailed helplessly in the air. The boat nearly capsized, but just as quickly, it returned to earth none the worse for the ride.

"YEEHAAAA!" screamed Steve.

Everyone yelled at the near catastrophe. Great fun!

Between bouts of excitement, we drifted through astounding geological beauty. Our journey carried us through dramatic layers of millions of years of sedimentation.

Major Powell wrote: "The limestone of this canyon is often polished, and makes a beautiful marble. The rocks are many colors—white, gray, pink, red, and purple with tints of saffron. It is with great labor that we make progress, meeting with many obstructions, running rapids, letting down our boats with lines from rock to rock, and sometimes carrying boats and cargoes around the bad places."

At 24 ½ Mile Rapid, we paid tribute to Bert Loper, 79, an old time river runner who died at that rapid in 1949. Sitting in the raft, I knew danger and death lurked just over the side of the rubber buttress, but here we passed a guy who actually MET his death on this rapid that we navigated. Bravo to Bert dying doing what he loved and especially at 79 years of age. It meant he had a full measure of life before passing on to the next great adventure. A lot of guys joke that they want to die in bed in the arms of a younger woman. But the fact is, most of us would rather die doing something heroic. Maybe not even heroic. Just doing something we love! That's the way I want to go—on the racquetball court, ski slope on a 25 inch powder day, at the end of the day, of course, or on the dance floor, or on a bike tour around the world.

When it's my time to go, I want to be filled up with so much life that I'm satisfied that I've done all I could do. I want to be sick of living and be ready to check out. One thing is for damned sure and that is, I won't be sitting on my rear-end watching TV. I won't be in a nursing home. I won't linger. Like Jack London said, "It is so much easier to live placidly and complacently. Of course, to live placidly and complacently is not to live at all…I live like a meteor in the sky…going places with a blazing tail… not a sleepy, comfortable planet…no, I will not prolong my life, but I will live every moment."

It's good for my spirit to know others who lived full measure. I remember my grandmother telling me, "You're burning the candle at both ends…you're always going MUCH too fast…slow down." She didn't realize that my candle is longer and my life speed is normal for me just as a Peregrine falcon's speed is normal for him and a donkey's is normal for him. When I finally check out, whether it be on this trip on Lava Falls Rapid (which could kill any of us) or I get killed in the car accident on the way home, I KNOW I did the best I could to live full measure. In my life, there are no ordinary moments. There's no need or time for being average.

What is 'the next great adventure'? When the great aviator of the Atlantic Ocean Charles Lindbergh died, he said, "I'm ready for the ultimate last flight into the next adventure." What did he mean?

I think I know. I think death means a return to nothingness with the possibility of renewal through some other flight plan. When I die, my body will go back to the earth. It will become inert again as in, 'ashes to ashes'. It will have no meaning and it will be as if it never existed. My energy known as 'Frosty' will dissipate into the universe without meaning or personality. It's why I will be cremated and have my ashes thrown on a ski run so I can ski for eternity. But no matter where my ashes go, I'll be picked up by a flower for sustenance and possibly be food for a bug that is food for a rodent who might be food for an eagle. At some point, I might be the eye of an eagle and be soaring across the sky; or I might stay a mouse. It doesn't matter because it could be anything creative and living, or my ashes might stay meaningless. No matter what, I won't ever be me again, ever in the universe.

We enjoy a onetime shot at living. I think life on this planet is a fluke, a cosmic joke, a meaningless miracle, but I'm going to keep squeezing the hell out of it with every waking moment. I chuckle at all those who think they are going on to some place like 'heaven', so they discount or put off their enjoyment of this 'real' life—the one they have here and now. Life! It's a ton of fun! Turn frustration into fascination; Never in neutral; Lean into life. When I do go, I'll go with a big grin on my face. I had a ball and danced with some beautiful women.

Down through 24 ½ Mile Rapid, we lived! Old Mr. Loper died. That's life! Let's get on with it. We floated through Jurassic, Mesozoic, and Pliocene eras. As we drifted further into the canyon, the sandstone walls rose to 2,500 feet.

At one point, we floated under a huge cave in the canyon wall about 200 feet up from the river. Ranger's blocked off Stanton's Cave as it was called because it held Indian artifacts and many had been looted.

At noon, we floated around a corner to see the canyon wall lit up with sparkling diamonds that seemed to be moving down a cliff face. Below them, a lush green garden with red flowers gave contrast to the red rocks dominating the area. The closer we got to it, the clearer it became. A giant geyser spouted clear water out of a red cliff wall. A Bridal Veil Falls rushed down the red rocks—creating a jungle of plants and flowers beneath it. Birds flew in to refuel their bodies with fresh water and bumble-bees danced among the flowers. We discovered a beautiful oasis in the middle of this sun-baked canyon desert!

"This is paradise," Sally said. "It's so beautiful…it's like a dream."

"Yeah," Julie said. "And you're in it. Vasey's Paradise!"

"Not a bad place to be," Gary said.

Major Powell wrote when he saw it, "The river turns sharply to the east and seems enclosed by a wall set with a million brilliant gems. As we approached, we found fountains bursting from the rock high overhead, and the spray in the sunshine forms the gems which bedeck the wall. The rocks are covered with mosses and ferns and many beautiful flowering plants. We named it Vasey's Paradise in honor of the botanist who traveled with us."

We filled the water jugs and prepared lunch on the rocks near the falls. Later, we rinsed the rocks and sand clean of all foods so as not to leave anything that might harm the animals or have them start depending on human food. The key to so many people moving through the wilderness was to "LEAVE NO TRACE!" So far, I had only picked up two pieces of litter. That wasn't bad, because usually, when I go backpacking and camping, I pick up dozens of pieces of trash. It never ceases to astound me that people can travel through such beauty and leave such ugliness in the form of cans, glass, paper and plastic.

At mile 33, we floated around a bend in the canyon to see Red Wall Cavern. HUGE describes it! On the bottom of a 2,000-foot canyon wall, the river had cut out an amazing amphitheater. Major Powell estimated that 50,000 people could be housed inside it. I'd estimate that 20,000 could fit into it.

From deep inside the amphitheater, the view megaphoned outward into a dramatic display of the river, canyon walls and sand. A rock concert would have been a hit in such a place.

Along the canyon, we drifted past large caverns in the walls that had water seeping through the cracks which created elegant columns with green plants growing and what looked like solariums on the sides of the cliffs.

Julie read her book. Gary sat back—lifeless under his river hat. He set the oars into the side of the boat. The other rafts floated up or down river from us. At that time, I looked around me. I 'saw' silence. An imminent quiet pervaded the canyon. As I sat there, it became profoundly evident to me that we had exited civilization and floated into the heart of nature's pulsing rhythms. Stillness! Heat! Quiet! A serene feeling settled into my ears, mind and body. The quiet reflected off the canyon walls. It bounced off the still surface of the water. It calmed me. I stood neck deep in 'river time'. No clocks, no news, no paper, no Brian Williams, no ads—only nature. The outside world might be on a tear, but on 'river time' we lived only the moment.

Johann Wolfgang Von Goethe, the great philosopher said, "Plunge boldly into the thick of life, and seize it where you will; it is always interesting."

We camped on a high pitched bank and took a hike up to Saddle Canyon. It took us 45 minutes with a gain of 600 feet. We hiked along a narrow path that led higher up the side of the canyon until it dropped back into another canyon and onto the floor of a little stream. We followed it along a verdant path of jungle with lizards scampering hither and yon. As the darkness neared, bats flitted about grabbing their evening cache of bugs. Steve saw a big lizard, which he pointed out to us. It must have been eight inches with colors like a Zebra. Soon, the canyon narrowed further and we made our way through rocks, sand and across the stream. Still, the walls closed in on us like a horror movie.

At the end, we waded through a rock-dammed mini-lake until we crawled over a VW-sized boulder and came to the end where we saw a 30 foot two pronged waterfall back against the fern covered rocks of the canyon. We took pictures with water pouring down on us as if we had a personal shower in the wilderness.

We hiked back to camp in the quickening darkness. Our view of the canyon provided one of mist and profiles. The sky turned gray with slashes of pink bouncing off the canyon walls from the ebbing sun. Far below, the eternal river—still worked its magic on those 1.7 billion-year-old rocks. Not only did the river work on the rocks, it worked its magic on my spirit.

Once again, the four women chefs worked their enchantment with a dinner fit for a bunch of kings. Four women to eight men! Gary cooked up steaks and baked potatoes on his grill. Salad refreshed us. Gary shared a surprise with a baked cherry pie from his Dutch Oven. I found it amazing that we feasted so well so many miles from a refrigerator! But Brenda carried a meal plan for three times a day. She worked it to perfection.

Strat pulled out his guitar and Wocnis grabbed his harmonica. Strat sang a song about love being like a toothache. While they sang, the conversations turned to the day's events. We became the sum of our experiences. Our daily adventures provided the grist for our conversations. After talking with all three Hall brothers, they convinced me that they were all riverboat captains in a former life or they were Vikings who voyaged around the world. The river flowed in their blood streams. Badger said he'd love to have enough money to be retired and raft every river around the globe. For an electrician, he carried a charge for living while floating on the river.

With each succeeding conversation, all our personalities emerged. Even Ivan, the quiet one, became a MOST engaging man when he started talking about his passion for the wilderness and animals. He wanted to start an Alpaca farm, and you know he will do it. His lady, Brenda, a physics and geology scientist showed great concern about the environment.

But then, a call wafted out over the din of the campfire, "Where are my dish fairies?" Brenda said.

Within moments, there could be heard a flapping of delicate wings somewhere on high the canyon walls. Three slight figures, one with a baseball cap, another with a jungle hat and another with no cap but the beginnings of a salt and pepper beard with a bit of a paunch around his mid section—SUDDENLY appeared out of the darkness. As they landed, a slight thud could be heard around camp from their tiny little feet hitting the sand. Being shy, they stood near the camp light hanging on a pipe secured to the kitchen table. Looking at them reminded one of the 'Three Stooges'. In their shorts, one featured long streamlined legs (that would be Steviness), the second had long skinny legs like a giraffe (Frostiness), and the third sported a short, stumpy, bowlegged pair (Rickiness). Their wings immediately folded back into their shoulders. Fairy dust sparkled on their childlike eyes and fell onto the sand.

"We're here, Brenda," they called softly.

"You know what to do," she said.

The Dish Fairies set about their tasks. Seconds seemed like minutes and minutes seemed like hours, but soon, the dishes magically washed clean and vanished into the kitchen box.

As if in a dream, the Dish Fairies wiped the tables clean and set the last dishcloth out to dry. Moments later, they spread their delicate wings and lifted off into the night to go where all Dish Fairies go after completing their jobs. But one of them muttered as he flew out of sight, "Hell, Steviness, that old witch Brenda isn't paying us enough for all this work."

"Shut up Rickiness," Frostiness said. "It's a livin' ain't it?!"

"I hate working," Rickiness said, as he flapped his wings vigorously to gain altitude. "In my next life, I'm gonna' be a lawyer."

CHAPTER 4—Canyon Sally makes wild rush through white water fury

> *"I often wonder what man will do with the mountains—that is, with their utilizable, destructible garments. Will he cut down all the trees to make ships and houses? If so, what will be the final and far upshot? Will human destructions like those of Nature—fire and flood and avalanche—work out a higher good, a finer beauty? Will a better civilization come in accord with obvious nature, and all this wild beauty be set to human poetry and song? And what is coming? What is the human part of the mountains' destiny?"*
>
> John Muir, 1875

"Who wants coffee?" Brenda called out in the morning. "Breakfast is served and you better get it before I put it away. We need to get an early start."

Brenda would have made an excellent company commander. She sets her priorities and moves people to action. We packed our gear and pushed onto the river early.

On this fourth day, I noticed something that I hadn't in the preceding days. We dove deeper into the Grand Canyon than ever before. The massive walls defied my imagination. The sky narrowed to a sliver of its former self.

Pulling out my copy of Powell's journal: "We find today, on comparing the readings of the barometers, that the walls are about 3,000 feet high—more than a half mile—and altitude difficult to appreciate from a mere statement of feet. The slope by which the ascent is made is not such a slope as is usually found in climbing a mountain, but one much more abrupt—often vertical for many hundreds of feet—so that the impression is given that we are at great depths, and we look up to see but a little patch of sky."

As I sat in the chair at the front of the boat, Gary prepared for running President Harding Rapid which the US Geological Survey party named in recognition of Harding's funeral.

Julie and I packed our reading materials and cameras for safe keeping and readied ourselves for the watery avalanche that would soak us to the bone. Into the raging water we rushed—water smashing into us, splashing us, and freezing us half to death. We shivered each time the wall of water hit, but quickly dried in the warm sunshine.

At lunch, we tied up five of our rafts to make a floating picnic. Brenda made sandwiches from pita bread. Master Chef! Along with the lunch time crowd, everyone spoke eloquently about the beauty we enjoyed.

After lunch, we broke up the party and again drifted as separate entities on that mighty river through time.

Mile after mile, the scenery changed, rearranged and enthralled us. Nature worked a lot of magic in 1.7 billion years. Intersecting canyons broke through the canyon walls on each side of us to create waterfalls. We discovered where the water had rushed over the crevasses, but, as we passed by, we saw only hot, dry rock.

As we floated along, a huge, perhaps three-story tall rock slab, and maybe 500,000 tons in weight, stuck up in the middle of the river like someone had shot an arrow into the sky and it had darted into the water. It fell from high above us by shearing off the canyon wall.

"I wouldn't have wanted to be here when that thing hit," Julie said.

"Me neither," I said.

"Do you want to try your hand at the oars?" Gary asked Julie.

"Sure."

Julie, ever the enthusiast, tried her hands at the oars. Gary and I had been rowing along for four days, but we were big strong guys. Gary's heavy wooden oars required a lot of muscle to move them. Before long, Julie decided that it wasn't much fun busting her tail trying to row the raft.

But later in the day, we watched Sally take the lighter fiberglass oars of Strat's boat and take it through the rapids. She looked like she was having the time of her life. In her journal that night, she wrote: "As I readied my oars and positioned the raft, my mind raced its own rapid of 'THE' rising roar of the approaching rapid—echoing the rising excitement AND anxiety rushing through my body! As I readied my oars and positioned the raft, my mind raced its own rapid of thoughts: "I don't know what I'm doing!" "What if I get my left and rights mixed up!" "I'm okay; it's more dangerous to be driving a car." Strat said, "The boat and current will generally carry us through just fine." Watch out for rocks, they're dangerous to get hung up on. Watch out for THAT rock!" "I'm sorry, I can't get them all." (My new rafting joke!). "How can you think of a joke at a time like this?!?" "Oh, my God." "What am I doing?"

"Ahhhhhhhhh...struggling to keep the oars in the water, grabbing for a pull to keep our raft heading straight into the giant waves, I know I don't want to get knocked over sideways. I don't want to be swimming in this freezing flood. Arms flexing, muscles pulling with all I've got, I hope it's enough to keep us alive. Whew, past a hole, and into more waves, but I see we're doing okay. I remember to look ahead. There is no 'down time' here in the rapids. I must stay with it or pay the price of inattention (and what about inexperience, I want to plead). We're heading right for a wall. "You're okay," Strat reassured me. "Just get ready to back paddle away, but wait 'til the last second to ride the current around." "Oh, my God, how can I do this?" I wonder. I'm exhausted by the tension, every moment a razor's edge of awareness and action.

"Wa... whoop! We did it! I did it! We made it! I can't believe I lived a whole lifetime getting through those last few minutes. How can anybody do this over and over again and not have their heart burst? Thank God for slow water!

"Frosty and Gary drifted up to us with cheers and congratulations. We celebrated another rapids run and I knew it was not even an important one. It was one I didn't dump us in though, and that was great. "Thank you, Ms. P. (the boat in whom I have great faith)," I said gratefully.

Rafting the Rolling Thunder

"Floating down stream now, feeling the reassuring warmth of the sun, life is simple and good. I continue to breathe and stay with this current that takes me around the endless carved corners in this Grand Canyon. Ahead lie mysteries, some buried deep in this ancient strata we dare drift through. What will I find? The canyon sentinels remain silent witnesses to my journey. "Stay tuned," the river whispers. And Canyon Sally whispers back, "I will."

As the sandstone met the limestone along our route, many caves had been hollowed out. Some featured springs dripping water from them and looked like giant solariums replete with majestic carvings profiled by green plants that grew into the canyon walls. They formed some of the most beautiful sights in Marble Canyon.

Powell saw them too as he wrote, "We have cut through the sandstones and limestones met in the upper part of the canyon and through one great bed of marble a thousand feet in thickness. In this formation above us, great numbers of caves are hollowed out, and carvings are seen which suggest architectural forms, though on a scale so grand that architectural terms belittle them. This great bed forms a distinctive feature of the canyon."

We hit Nankoweap Rapid. Or, should I say, the rapid HIT us! White water drenched us, over-powered us, and thrilled us. Nothing less than a SLAP, nature's style, in the face! From mile 52 through 53, we rock and rolled through seven huge rapids that kept us flying from one side of the river to the other. The tongue ran either 'river left' or 'river right'. If you've ever seen one of those movies where the good guy knocks the bad guy down the stairs and he tumbles until he hits the bottom—that was us! We tumbled down seven staircases of rapids that could care less whether we lived or died. But I got the feeling that they awaited us in a most devious way, you know, trying to spill us out of our little rubber rafts. Who would be the first to be thrown into the torrent of white water?

At that point, tan canyon walls swept vertically into the sky. The only way to describe it would be to walk under a city skyscraper in down town Denver or New York City—walk up to a building like the Empire State Building—and simply look up. At first, you would see the stone, windows and glass of the building, but soon, your vision blurs into the many layers rising upward into the sky until you only see a 'form' of rock rising into the clouds. That's what we saw that day. The rock started at the water line and climbed into the sky until we couldn't see it anymore. At the top, it vanished into blue sky.

But around each bend in the river, we floated along a watery conveyor belt that carried us through billions of years of erosion. One minute we floated backward and the next, sideways, and the next, forward—yet, all along, like a spinning cup at a county fair ride, in slow motion. The grandeur repeated itself in endless varieties of new and more formidably creative measures. A quiet symphony played that only our eyes 'heard'. It visually and spiritually mesmerized all of us every single day of the trip.

While I sucked in all the sights of the canyon, the river carried us downward into its deepest secrets. We rushed over Kwagunt Rapid past Malgosa Canyon into 60 Mile Rapid and stopped at the Little Colorado River intersection. There, the white, chalky water of the smaller

Rafting the Rolling Thunder

river mingled with the clear green waters of the big river. It did create a bit of clouding in the clear water, but soon, it cleared again. Steve and Brenda dove into the Little Colorado which swept them downstream. The 100 degree temperatures urged all of us to jump into the cold water.

At this juncture, the river swept along faster this day and carried us over many rapids. We passed Carbon Creek and into Lava Canyon.

Powell wrote, "We are now ready to start our way down the Great Unknown. We have but a month's rations remaining. We have an unknown distance yet to run, and an unknown river to explore. With some eagerness and some anxiety and some misgivings we enter the canyon below and are carried along by the swift water."

His journal entries gave me pause. What if I was floating down this river with no idea of the dangers ahead? Sure, I'm brave now, but I have an idea of what's to come and the equipment to succeed. Those men lived by their wits and a courage that I cannot know at this time of civilization. It's true; we have it so easy.

We reached Tanner Rapid for another tumble down the stairs of five separate and very wild rapids that were squeezed between narrow canyon walls. The excitement of watching each of the rafts run the rapids was as much fun as finding ourselves in the roiling waters. The 'thrill' of it was the ever-present possibility that anyone could capsize. We shared the thrill of victory and the very real agony of being dumped into the freezing waters of the Colorado that kept our attention. Plus, the potential of being pummeled by the rocks and rollers that would throw us around like rag dolls in a hurricane if we fell into the drink.

We stopped at Cardenas Creek for camp. A Spaniard named Don Garcia Lopez de Cardenas became the first non-Indian to report seeing the Grand Canyon in 1540. If his spirit lives somewhere up there in the big unknown, he can smile at knowing his name continues in perpetuity.

Dinner filled us to the gills. Nothing like a wonderful meal to top off the day! But of course, Brenda called the Dish Fairies of the Grand Canyon at the end of the meal.

"Dish Fairies," Brenda called out. "Front and center."

As we sat in our lawn chairs, Rick looked at me and I looked at Steve, and then we all looked at each other. The party—ended! We spread our wings and dutifully gathered the dishes, cups, silverware, and pots and pans. Steve boiled a pot of water while Rick gathered two tubs full from the river. I scraped the leftover food into a plastic bag. Rick poured a cap-full of bleach into the final rinse. We had to leave all dishes in it for 60 seconds. After drying them and putting them away, we filtered the wash water through a screen and placed the food particles in the garbage bag. Everything gleamed spotless when we finished.

It took all three of us to complete the task each night. Everyone else got to sit around and talk about the day's experiences. But for the Dish Fairies, we had to complete our task before being let off the chain of responsibility. Under the starlight in dishwashing section, the conversation always turned to any number of things, but almost without fail, it turned to sex. As little as middle-aged men get sex, we might as well have not even talked about it. But we couldn't help thinking about it.

Once we completed the dishes, the Dish Fairies of the Grand Canyon spread their delicate wings and lifted into the night. As we rose higher into the black sky, we heard Strat strumming on his guitar and Wocnis mouthing his harmonica. Badger, Ivan and Gary talked about the day's adventures. The ladies had their own conversations going in a round robin. Everyone wore shorts with T-shirts and sandals. The hot day had turned into a warm night. We witnessed a perfectly quiet scene framed by the river in front and the bushy trees surrounding the campsite with a base of white sand. And, high in back of them, the grand magic of the canyon walls played in the starlight. I looked over at Rickiness, his delicate wings fluttering effortlessly, "not a bad night," I said.

"Yes, my friend," he said. "Not a bad night, but I broke a nail on the last pot."

"You know," Steviness said, fluttering. "It's always something if you're a dish fairy."

CHAPTER 5—Fear has a funny way of changing your intestines

> *"Life is a dog and then you die...not so...life is a joyous dance through the daffodils beneath cerulean blue skies. And then? I forget what happens next. And where have the years gone? Why, into the usual vices of the romantic realist: into sloth and melancholy, love and marriage and the begetting of children, into the strenuous maneuvers of earning a living without living to earn, into travel and play and music and drink and talk and laughter, into saving the world—but saving the world was only a hobby. Into watching cloud formations fly across our planetary skies. I don't regret a moment of it."*
> Ed Abbey

We shoved off at 8:30 a.m. because Brenda insisted we get an early start on a big day of more miles. Gary grabbed the oars while Julie and I made ourselves comfortable. Thus, Julie began her last day on the river, as she would hike out at the Bright Angel Trail. We started the morning at mile 71.

Out in the middle of the river, Wocnis had set up his pink umbrella, but had dropped it into the current. It floated upside down and away from his raft. Within seconds, he leaped into the 47 degree water and swam out to retrieve his umbrella. No doubt he froze his cheeks off.

Very soon, the river narrowed still further until we dumped into Unkar Rapid. That rapid swung around a corner which caused a hellacious side flow from the water bouncing off the sheer rock wall. Gary heaved on his oars to keep the boat from colliding with the cliff face. All the while, we yelled and cheered the swirling wildness around us.

Further down the canyon, the emery board colored sandstone walls grew closer and closer. A kind of immediacy of the cliff walls overcame us as we raced over Nevills Rapid.

Several miles later, Gary said, "We're coming up on Hance Rapid. This one is going to be interesting."

"What does that mean?" I asked, noting his obvious concern.

"People have died on this one," Gary said.

This time, the roar of the rapids took on more power. The canyon opened up and the river swung wide to the right. All the other boats ahead of us pulled to 'river left' to scout out the rapid. Heretofore, all the sounds, the roar of the rapid meant a lot of fun. It meant a roller coaster ride. Why should this be any different?

I climbed over some rocks and up a hill. At the top, the view of Hance sent shivers down my spine. It measured over 1,000 feet long with a 50-foot drop on the incline. Huge, and I do mean, HUGE 50-ton boulders waited like the devil had planted them in strategic spots along the rapid. It looked like the inclined face of a pinball machine. Huge swirling white water roared off the sides of the boulders that looked like giant VW bus-sized bowling pins, but in this case, no bowling ball could knock those babies over. A raft could get caught in any of the 'holes' and be dumped in a second. The contents of the raft could be thrown out whether humans or cargo. Once out into the 'devil's playing field', a human could become the pinball and the 50 ton rock 'pins' would get their revenge on the ball.

My guts churned up in my stomach. I turned to Gary who conversed with Wocnis, who talked to Ivan.

"I'm going to run the right side," Ivan said. "It looks like deeper water and an easier path through the boulders."

"It's deeper, but look at the calmer water along the left side," Wocnis said.

"Hey, you guys," I said. "It looks like a sheet of white churning ice to me and none of it looks like anyone could live through that white rage."

"Don't get too excited," Gary said. "We can do this."

From my perspective, it was a 1,000-foot long suicide pinball alley with no escape—and we could become pinballs with no mercy shown by the water. All that would have to happen was the raft to hit a boulder and flip, and our bodies would become mincemeat. For the first time since I crawled through live ammunition fire during my Army basic training in the infantry, I felt fear. NO, not 'felt' fear—my mind 'poured' FEAR into every cell in my body like a waitress pours hot, steaming coffee into your cup. The vapors surrounded me, almost debilitating me. I had to go to the bathroom. I could die in those rapids.

The same nervous energy I felt at the beginning of a triathlon—where my entire body tingled with adrenaline—I felt at that moment.

We stood atop the hill while Ivan, Brenda and Cindy floated into the tongue on 'river right'. He hit a couple of rocks and then, dropped over a huge wave and got stuck in the hole. He got pulled forward into the hole and then sucked backward toward the boulder that created the 'hole'. As he pulled on his oar, it broke out of its oarlock. Brenda moved to the high side with Cindy and they managed to escape dumping the raft. Ivan had only one oar to work the rapids. He looked helpless and out of control. Ivan scrambled like a man possessed to get the oar back into the slot. The boat pulled away from the hole behind the rock and he spun down river. His boat bounced from one rock to another until, thankfully and mercifully, he pulled through the remaining white water and back into the quiet green of the Colorado River.

"My God!" I exclaimed. "He made it!"

Everyone cheered!

Strat and Sally followed. The veteran river rafter floated 'river left' through the entanglement of slower water but more obstacles. Amazingly, he maneuvered down the boulders and popped into the quiet water without much fanfare.

I still felt scared. Julie wasn't fazed. She had so much trust in Gary and had never experienced being thrown from a raft, that she didn't know enough to sense the danger. She did say one thing to me that showed me what a tremendous competitor and athlete she was, "Why not think about the positives…it's what we came for."

"You're right," I said.

"Sure," she said. "It's better to think of all the good things…Gary's experience, a good boat, many people have done it successfully, and we just saw Ivan and Strat run it." "You're right," I said.

I looked at Gary, "If you're confident to go down that hell hole, then your confidence is my confidence."

"We'll make it," he said, his many years as a boatman showing on his face.

"I'm with you," I said, still sick to my stomach.

We returned to Gary's boat where Julie and I put on our helmets. If I was going to be a pinball boy, my head would be reasonably protected.

Instead of the excitement that churned inside me the previous four days of running rapids, I did not feel the 'fun' of the moment. Call it a bad hair day or 'I want my mommy', but this kid felt fear. No smile crossed my face. I held on and hoped for a 'safe' run.

As all those emotions zig-zagged through my mind, I stopped for a moment and reflected: What the hell was I worried about? I had faced two grizzly bears in Alaska years before. I'd been caught in a blizzard in the Bolivian Andes at 16,000 feet and nearly froze to death. I could have been run over by any million trucks or cars in my bicycling rides around the world. I could have fallen through a crevasse and still be frozen to death in an icy grave in Antarctica. Death could have surely grabbed me in the Outback of Australia from heat stroke or lack of water. One guy in a group behind me DID die on a climb through the Himalayas near Mount Everest. It could just as easily been me. So, what the hell was I afraid of? I should already be dead from all the adventures I've lived in the past 30 years. Then, I realized that it was in my mind. Maybe that's what stops most people from 'sucking the marrow' out of life. Not me, damn it! I'm rafting down that rapid, live or die, and laughing all the way. Well, maybe not laughing today, but I was going to run that river.

"Crap," I muttered to myself. "You're a damned sniveling coward. Get a grip! This is adventure. It's not supposed to be comfortable. Go out and live it."

Gary set the boat up sideways on 'river left'. We swept along on the still waters of the tongue until we hit the chute where the water began its drop into the rock field. Gary put us into the center of two 50-ton boulders that resembled VW's stood on their bumpers. The ones behind them proved the size of Cadillacs. Everywhere, furious, raging white water boiled and roared at us. We headed into the frothy depths of white water hell.

We dropped into a maelstrom of turbulence. We crashed through, but immediately, a HUGE boulder presented itself. Several rocks resembling the fangs on a grizzly cut through the water threatening to slice our boat into bacon strips. The water roared like a dozen grizzlies howling in our ears from only inches away. Wouldn't anyone be terrified if a dozen grizzlies were about to eat him or her? Okay, I admit it; I'm a chicken with white tail feathers.

Gary deftly cranked on the oars and brought us to the near side of another VW bus-sized boulder. We smashed into it with the front of the raft, but Gary suddenly reefed on the oars and with mighty strokes, he cranked the oars to turn us 180 degrees where we spun into the hole of another rock. His arms bristled with the strain on the oars. The 'hump' of water bolted the raft skyward, again like a bucking bronco. There was no way to go around it as we rode the hump and crashed downward into the turbulence on the other side.

All this action continued in silence as I avoided yelling or cheering. Julie probably took my cue, as she remained quiet. I hope I didn't ruin it for her because she always cheered the loudest. But I couldn't help my quiet, because at any moment, we could run up a rock and be flipped or pinned. If we got pinned, the water would be like a 50-ton sledgehammer smashing us against a rock. If we flipped, we'd be at the mercy of pinball alley.

At that moment, I could do nothing. But our ace in the hole—Gary! His talents, strength and skill worked with whatever the river threw at him.

Could we die?

Yes!

Might we live?

More than likely!

But every year, a certain number of people die or get hurt on the river. That's the one thing about nature; it doesn't give a damn whether you live or you die…break a leg…laugh or cry. Nature makes no apologies. Why should it? Around the planet at any given moment, every kind of animal is at risk for its life—either by being eaten, accident, disease, violence or old age.

My time will come. It could be today, tomorrow or 30 years from now, but my time will come. Before it comes, or while it is coming, I'm packing it all in to the max. Not a day goes by that I allow to be wasted.

At the end of the run, we hit a six-foot hole, which turned into a wall of water three feet thick. Julie and I became Gary's windshield, and at the same time, two hapless bugs that felt a distinct splat as our bodies got hit by the wall of water. She suddenly laughed and I hollered because we knew we were through the most dangerous part of the rapid. Even if we flipped out, we'd be swimming through deep water with no boulders to grind us into shredded cheese.

From that point, I gained incredible respect for the finesse and skill Gary possessed at the helm.

Moments after successfully running Hance Rapid, I remembered the quote by Thoreau: "I came to live deliberately in the woods…to suck the marrow out of life. I wanted to live life with consciousness and maintain alertness to every creative moment."

As we headed down the river between rapids, astounding changes of geography increased our wonder. Brenda announced that we had descended to rock that was 1.7 billion years old.

Some of the rock thrust out along the river in horizontal multiples of two-inch layers that looked like the feathers on an eagle. Other layers resembled a birthday cake. Still higher, some layers shot vertical lines skyward like skyscrapers along New York's Madison Avenue. At the top, still more ancient sand dune mountains of compacted rock "T'd" off on the vertical layers which created an amazing contrast when seen from a mile below.

In addition, colored rock filled fissures within the layers and, in many cases, looked like it had seeped in like some form of lava.

Sometimes, a huge chunk of black rock projected up into the stone colored rocks like someone had shot a 50-ton arrow out from the middle of the planet and it stuck pointing skyward. Just incredible!

As the afternoon sun glistened off some of the pure black polished stone, I realized we witnessed veins of exposed coal. Catastrophic upheaval followed us along this journey through time. It felt like being in a Jurassic Park movie where a huge dinosaur might appear around the next bend.

Sockdolager Rapid and Grapevine tested Julie. She had switched boats over to Wocnis' raft. We watched her maneuver the speedy craft through the wild whitewater. She aced both rapids with the aplomb of a river veteran. Her canyon-wide smile said it all.

Sadly, at Kaibab, Julie gave Gary a big hug and kissed him good-bye, and hiked out of the canyon on the Bright Angel Trail. She returned to work. She spent her time on the river well. After eating lunch, we launched back into the river.

We passed Cheyava Falls where water exploded out of solid rock and cascaded in a series of falls before flowing into the river.

At mile 90, we faced a humongous cataract at Horn Creek. The rollers reached ten feet high. They proved big, ugly, and scary. Two boats dropped into the wild water without incident. Wocnis, Badger, Steve and Rick raced through the rolling thunder. In front of us, Ivan,

Cindy and Brenda began their descent on the deep quiet of the tongue 'river right'. Ivan pressed right to miss a huge boulder and then pulled back to the left to hit the center.

I stood up as Gary looked over the terrain on the other side of the raft.

"Looks big," I said.

"It IS big!" he said. "Ivan is one of the best boatmen I know. I think I'll follow his route."

At that moment, Ivan swept down past the boulder, but instantly lost control as his raft slid sideways and turned completely around. Before he could do anything, his stern rushed up a 10-foot wall of water. Cindy looked back to see a tidal wave of green rolling over Ivan's backside. The 16-foot raft with all its gear hung for a moment in the grasp of the rising wave, and suddenly, like the Titanic, it broke loose from the wave and somersaulted downward. The boat tossed Ivan into the air like a slingshot. Both Cindy and Brenda plummeted downward and into the icy green white water.

The raft plunged downward behind Ivan and smashed upside down into the water. At that moment, compressed water pushed Ivan to the floor of the river by the massive forces being piled against his body. The water ripped a sandal off his foot. He struggled against being ground up on the bottom and trying to find his raft. The raft trapped both women when it fell on them. They struggled in a world of bubbles and swirling, freezing water. For them—stuffed headfirst into nature's Maytag washing machine at FULL agitation. Gravel cut into Brenda's legs and scraped her arms. Cindy, in shock, struggled out from under the boat and swam for the surface. She popped up from the water and Brenda's head appeared seconds later. Ivan swam to his raft and the threesome hung on as the current pushed them over against the canyon walls 'river left'.

Within seconds, we too, glided down the tongue of Horn Creek. The water dropped steeply which led to a big wave about to greet us. In front and 'river right', a huge wave more than nine feet high rose up out of the river. But what was even more sobering was the 'hole' it created behind it. The hole dropped nine feet and then the ensuing wave climbed to ten feet, maybe twelve feet. To the left of it, another set of seven-foot rollers and a series of five big ones awaited us. We saw what had happened to Ivan.

"We'll have to go into the right of the big rock, then pull hard to the left to stay out of the hole," Gary said.

"We've got to miss that first rock on the left before we can pull to the left to miss that monster on the right," I said.

"Sure enough," Gary said.

We braced ourselves. Although not afraid anymore, I saw behemoth waves appear as we dropped into the white fury. I stared at a wall of white. Gary quickly eased past the left rock and started toward the BIG ONE on the right. But before we got there, Gary heaved hard on the oars twice. His efforts pulled us away from the hole, but not before I glanced over to see an eight-foot deep drop on the backside of that rock that then shot like a runaway elevator to a ten-foot heavy wall of water. Had we dropped into that hole and tried to climb the wall, we would have never made it and would have flipped like a Texas tumbleweed into the 'hole' like Ivan had.

No matter! We still faced six-foot holes in a series almost like a machine gun rattling off some rounds. I stood up in front of the raft and hung on to the bow straps.

Sure enough, the boat sank into the hole and I saw solid green water quickly turning into white madness. It hit me at the crest and smashed over my body like Tiger Woods trying a one wood and going for an eagle on a par five. You know how hard he hits that ball to drive it 300 yards? It knocked me back. Before I could recover, we crested the roller and dropped on the way down. But the next roller sported a lateral wave cracking into it from the left, which caused a double crest 'reflex' wave. It collided with the front and side of the bow. Again, I resembled a bug on the windshield as the raging wall of foot thick water crashed into me with relentless fury. I recoiled back to my seat and grabbed the side straps because the next wave looked even higher.

As we dove into it, I looked back at Gary who remained as calm as the eye of a hurricane. He had to be.

I turned my attention to the next dive into that hellhole of water. This roller grew tighter, so, as the front of the 16-foot raft rammed into the bottom of the hole, the front end buckled back as it hit a dead end. It threw me backward and my feet shot skyward. Just as quickly, the raft dove and quickly followed upward. Again, I saw all white and all blue. On the next drop, the boat glided to the bottom...then headed skyward...exploding through the white water like someone had thrown a stick of dynamite at the front of our boat.

From there, the rollers diminished until they eased into roiling water. I stood up and immediately bailed eight inches of water off the bottom.

"Let's get over to their boat," Gary said.

To our left, Ivan, Brenda and Cindy had washed over to a rocky cove. Ivan stood on the bottom of his raft while Cindy and Brenda hauled themselves out of the water and stood on a boulder.

"You all right?" we yelled.

They gave us the thumbs up sign.

Gary rowed over to them and Strat and Sally followed us. We pulled into the boulder and secured the rafts with ropes.

"No one hurt?" Gary asked.

"We're fine," Brenda said.

Ivan stood atop his boat with two lines across the port side. Gary, Strat and I secured the lines with Ivan's help. Three lines were tied into place before we tried to turn the raft over.

"One, two, three, PULL!" Gary said.

The big raft didn't budge.

Across the river, Wocnis and Steve along with Badger and Rick paddled up river in an eddy high enough to attempt a crossing over the current and help us. About 40 yards upstream, the rocks blocked them. Both Badger and Wocnis heaved hard on the oars as they sent their boats into the whitewater, but each time, were swept past us.

They tried again and I threw out a line to try and catch them, but that too, failed.

We had two choices—either let the boat float upside down and guide it to a shore landing and turn it over there, or enlist the three women with four men to pull. We strained mightily until the entire raft first rose to a vertical position, and finally with more reefing on the lines, we eased it back into the upright position in the water. Ivan checked all his gear. His securing efforts paid off. Even though no one wants to flip a boat, everything on the raft must be rigged everyday as if the boat would flip.

We floated back into the current and pitched camp a short time later. A brazen crimson burned across the heavens while the last sunlight lit the tan cliffs above us into a firewall of burning embers. Shadows crept up the cliffs while darkness slipped into the Grand Canyon. The first bats darted hither and yon along the river's surface. The Big Dipper jumped out of a corner of the sky and wedged between two cliffs at the east end of the valley as if it were meant to be framed by the ancient rocks.

To get a feeling of ancient, The Big Dipper has occupied the sky for billions of years. The canyon rock, as Brenda stated, was 1.7 billion years old. In a sense, we had dropped more than a billion years through time on our descent through eternity.

As I sat there watching the endless current of the ancient river, a sense of wonder and awe transformed my mind. Only 141 years ago, J.W. Powell, a one armed military man and a band of nine comrades explored this canyon. Perhaps a few rocks have fallen in that time, but no major changes have taken place. Maybe a million more years will pass before much change will be perceptible. I will be gone in another 30. This place will be here another five billion years.

That night, we celebrated Cindy's 50th birthday. Rick broke out the champagne and we toasted to her good health and vital life. It interested me in that she was two thirds finished with her life. In another blink, she'd be 60 and moments later, 70. Most of us exit before 80.

It sobered me to realize that a human life begins and ends as quickly as a Mayfly's eighteen hour existence when brought into comparison with eternity.

As my friend Dan Millman said, "There are no ordinary moments. Make the most out of every second you are alive."

CHAPTER 6—Satori while screaming at the top of your lungs

> *"Something will have gone out of us as a people if we ever let the remaining wilderness be destroyed…if we pollute the last clean air and dirty the last clean streams and push our paved roads through the last of the silence."*
> Wallace Stegner

Dawn breaks with effortless quiet over this ancient canyon. It pushes away the darkness with the coming of the sun's rays creeping across the sky. The first hint looms on the eastern horizon with a faint glow invading the blackness above me. The looming profiles of the canyon change from meaninglessness to color and form. I change from sleep to awareness. I hear a few voices as my mates slog their way to the 'Groover'. Chirping birds break the silence along the river.

Gary invited me to sleep on his boat last night. He's a river man. He's given me an incredible gift by taking me on this trip with him. Brenda registered the permit and she invited me. It took her eight years for the permit. I'll always be indebted to her. Now, it takes ten to fifteen years to obtain a raft permit on the Colorado River through the Grand Canyon.

Gary and I stretched out across the two bench seats on both ends of the raft. We had rolled out our air mattresses, sleeping bags and used the life vests for pillows. We fell asleep under a starlit sky with shooting stars slicing through the blackness. The water quietly curled around the raft beneath us while it rendered a most tranquil way to fall asleep under the night sky.

Next morning, pancakes made a hot breakfast along with steaming coffee and tea.

We maneuvered the rafts into fast moving multiple rapids from mile marker 90. We hit one rapid and then another. I bailed water like a madman with each rapid as they repeatedly pounded gallons of water into the boat on each run.

We passed Trinity Creek and later, Salt Creek. It amazed me to be traveling through this rocky, hot desert (100 degrees), with nothing growing except bushes on the banks of the river, and suddenly see a clear creek pouring its sparkling water out of some nameless canyon.

By now, I felt pretty well versed in the power of the river. One slip could upend us in a heartbeat. From having fun, we could be sucked into the jaws of danger and even death in milliseconds.

Gary handed the oars over to me.

"Time to test your skills," he said.

"Piece of cake," I said.

I worked through smaller rapids the day before. Each rapid taught a lesson. Gary called, "river left" or "river right" when the main flow of the river worked a pathway left of center or right in the riverbed. I maneuvered the craft into the 'tongue' or the main flow of the water. From there, I swung the boat, like an arrow, straight down the middle. Even the slightest deviation from dead center could swing the boat sideways where it would flip from the hydro pressure built up in each wave.

With the first rapid, a six-foot roller awaited. It wasn't hard to thread the needle of the first one, but as a rookie, the boat got away from me and 'flew' out of the water, which gave my oars the appearance of bony wings. Except, they weren't meant to oar the 'air'! They needed to be in the water. The raft took off to the left 45 degrees. Gary pointed at a large boulder just under the surface. It could rip the bottom of the raft to shreds. "TURN US!" he yelled. I dug the oars deep and pulled. The boat straightened out just in time to hit the second seven-foot wall of water head on. The nose smashed through a ton of liquid ice that exploded all over the bow and into Gary.

The next roller looked like the Godzilla of waves—deep green and thick—like the tongue of a T-Rex. The wave grew heavy, like the movie "Perfect Storm" and became more ominous as the boat rushed down the back side and headed into the next tempest.

I lowered both oars into the water to steady the raft. For a moment, as big as the wave was, a shot of fear ripped through my body like someone had stuck my hand into a campfire and held it there. Just as quickly, my attention pointed to that one single monster in front of me.

It's called 'satori', a moment of perfect living—where a challenge engages all of your mind, body and spirit into a single focus. You live in the 'here and now'. It matters little what the challenge! Richard Bach with Jonathan Livingston Seagull called it, "The perfect speed." Sometimes, when you're in the middle of 'it', you're scared shitless. At other moments, you're screaming at the top of your lungs with wild abandonment. It can be joy or it can be fear. It WILL move you in ways you never expect. It can be cowardice and it can become courage.

Is that what life is all about? Do we get a smooth roll on the front end of a wave? On the front end of our lives? But soon after, life throws big, honking, saber rattling, horrific obstacles into our paths?! What do we do when that happens? Many of us go into denial or run like crazy, but in the end, life forces us to meet the challenge. If we try to turn away, life will turn and step in front of us. Sooner or later, reality catches up. For many, we shove our lives right into the face of death almost asking for a consequence, i.e., drugs, booze, over eating, et al. For others, it's endless TV or other forms of non-involvement. It's tricky to find a balance. Nature offers balance!

I met naturalist Gwen Frostic in the later years of her life. She said, "Let's just wander here and there, like leaves floating in the autumn air and look at the common things, stones on the beach, flowers turning into berries; from the winds we'll catch a bit of that wondrous feeling that comes, not from seeing, but from being part of nature."

As with these monster waves on the Colorado River, nature does not disappoint. I gulped my fear and moved the raft into position. Moments later, a wall of water bashed Gary and poured 20 gallons into the boat. With that much water, our raft 'became' the river.

The next roller lessened until we hit roiling, boiling water. Gary grabbed a bucket and began heaving water overboard. He looked back with a grin, "Good job." My reaction on that point was a big smile. "Thanks!"

You know, we all need to be praised and appreciated no matter what our tasks. The older I become, I am convinced that we're all a bunch of little kids in 'grown up' clothing. Remember when you said, "Look at me Mommy…look at me Daddy."

It's no different as we get older. The nicest way to make a fellow human being's day is to pay them a compliment. I do it all the time. Each time, it blows me away at the reactions I receive. When I compliment the grocery store cashier by saying, "Gosh, those ear rings look beautiful on you." Her big smile makes my day. Sometimes it looks like they just won the million-dollar lottery. Their smiles provide joyful energy for my spirit. Go out and try it. You'll be delighted.

That night, we camped on a sandbar. Everyone ate dinner, but I was too exhausted to shovel any food into my mouth. I climbed into my tent to read.

Thoreau said, "We need the tonic of the wildness—to wade sometimes in marshes where the bittern and the meadow-hen lurk, and hear the booming of the snipe; to smell the whispering sedge where only some wilder and more solitary fowl builds her nest."

Thankfully, the other two Dish Fairies gave me the night off.

CHAPTER 7—Across the sky as if pulled by chariots of fire

> *"Tentative efforts lead to tentative outcomes. Therefore, give yourself fully to your endeavors. Decide to construct your character through excellent actions and determine to pay the price of a worthy goal. The trials you encounter will introduce you to your strengths. Remain steadfast...and one day you will build something that endures; something worthy of your potential."*
>
> Epictetus
> Roman teacher

Both Gary and Wocnis slept on their rafts last night. Those guys must have river water running through their arteries. In another life, Wocnis captained Stephan Crane's ***The Open Boat***, and Gary may have been the inspiration for Hemmingway's ***The Old Man and the Sea.***

Funny how their conversations took place on the rafts! Last night, they talked about the rapids, and the day before—who ran them well and which ones fared poorly. Ivan paid ignominiously for his flip.

"On Hance, Ivan was a victim after he lost his oar on the first hole," Wocnis said. "Lucky to get out alive after doing that rendition of a Texas tumble weed on Horn Creek."

Ivan stood silent as was his way and took another drag on his pipe.

"You would have had to have been there," he said, matter of fact. "The hole ripped my oar out of the lock and out of my hand…."

Meanwhile, within the circle of lawn chairs, Strat strummed on his guitar as he belted out a song he had written:

"Oh well, a toothache reminded me of you,
It hurt me just like you used to do;
The love that we had has now gone bad,
And there's nothing that a doctor can do.

Everything's inflated these days,
Cuz love don't pay no minimum wage;
It was costing too much, had to lay off the stuff,
And I keep getting older day by day.

If another ever hurt me like you,
Tell you just what I'm going to do;
Put her on a track with a hot dog on her back;
And call out the state militia, too.

I'd climb a mountain for your love,
Way up to the silky clouds above;
Going to slip and slide down the great divide,
To the Colorado River mud."

Strat's song revealed lost love. My, my, haven't we all been there! Anyone who hasn't suffered from a broken heart? It's in every country and western song ever sung. We humans express our misery and celebrate our joy.

It's funny about life, but we talk about our reality. Fishermen talk about the big one that got away. A river rafter talks about the ten-foot rollers that pounded him. The skier relates a two-foot powder day. Motocross riders talk about their 'rad' day on the course. We find pleasure in the story-telling after the dramatic moment. The greater the moment, the greater the story!

Powell wrote, "It was especially cold in the rain tonight. The little canvas we had was rotten and useless; the rubber ponchos were all lost; we have not a blanket apiece. So, we built a fire; but the rain, coming down in torrents, extinguished it, and we sat up all night on the rocks, shivering, and are more exhausted by the night's discomfort than by the day's toil."

No doubt, Powell's exploration was much tougher than ours because of equipment. Our tents, air mattresses and sleeping bags were state of the art and very comfortable in any weather.

We shoved off after a bagel breakfast.

It amazed me how two cooking tables, stoves, gas grill, six tents, 12 chairs, the Groover and a dozen dry bags along with large water containers made it onto the rafts each day. But, by 9:00 a.m., five fully loaded boats, 12 faces and all our gear floated into the unknown.

We soon crashed into a roller coaster, bumper-car rally ride that lathered us in constant rapids. Gary stood up for each rapid to survey the best approach. We saw the other boats crashing, blasting, rising, falling and vanishing into the white water. Soon, we too headed into the violent cataract with spray flying and huge gobs of water pouring into the boat. As soon as the raft made it through the rapid, Gary said, "Bail with vigor!" That meant we headed into more rapids. We flew through Hermit, Boucher, Crystal, Tuna Creek, Sapphire and Ruby Rapid while enjoying an exhilarating ride.

At noon, we stopped at Shinumo Rapid where we waded up a narrow clear stream to a 15-foot waterfall with a pool beneath it. Everyone took showers and splashed around like a bunch of kids on playground monkey bars.

It never ceases to amaze me that we adults are just as enthusiastic as kids, and as is so often the case, we are only little kids in grown up bodies—but we still express the bliss and glee of getting wet in a waterfall.

In the stream flowing from the falls, we pumped 20 gallons through a filter to give ourselves safe drinking water. Everyone pitched in to help.

Back on the river, we drifted slowly through deep water and vertical cliff canyon walls. Four thousand feet above us and 1.7 billion years of time rendered great church cathedrals that dwarfed Notre Dame and gave a powerful expression of the Creator's embroidery.

"This is beyond fantastic," I said.

Brenda, floating close by, said, "This is God's handiwork just for your pleasure."

Obviously, God had plenty of time on Her hands because a person could sit in one place for a hundred years and not see much change or even a rock fall.

We stopped at a place called Elves Chasm. A short hike up a steep rock canyon brought us through a flower garden near a crystal clear stream with green moss growing in pools and each pool led to another more beautiful one until it, too, led to a 12-foot waterfall with ferns growing out of the rock.

At the end, the stream led to a large rock pool where a 30-foot waterfall lined with red flowers and lush green ferns awaited weary hikers. We dove in and got our pictures taken in front of the falls. Gary and I snapped shots of us falling into the clear pool. Again, the river offered more magic, more unexpected beauty.

But for some reason, this day, nature wanted to overload us with splendor!

John Muir said, "This grand show is eternal. It is always sunrise somewhere; the dew is never all dried at once; a shower is forever falling; vapor is ever rising. Eternal sunrise, eternal sunset, eternal dawn and gloaming, on sea and continents and islands, each in its turn, as the round earth rolls."

Around the next bend in the river, a gargantuan amphitheater with 4,500-foot walls of red and tan rock, the color of baked ham and white turkey breast and a mile across—greeted our stunned eyes. Out in front of the concave wall, a towering spire of rock, 2,000 feet high and resembling the Empire State Building—stood as if it were the light filament to the world's largest red reflector on the world's largest lighthouse.

"My God, Gary," I said. "Would you look at that!"

"It's called Explorer's Monument," he said.

"Can you imagine Powell and his men seeing that for the first time?" I said.

"They would not have any reference for something so incredibly massive," Gary said. "I hardly have enough room in my eyes to take it all in myself."

This place! Definitely off the scale of normal! As we drifted down river, I could not take my eyes off the spectacle in front of me. It's one of the most awesome sights I have ever encountered.

On a smaller scale, we drifted down past two, then four mountain goats. They stood 40 meters above us—perched on a rock cliff. Two rams proudly displayed their huge horn racks while the ewes licked the rocks for salt deposits.

Speaking of wildlife, we enjoyed a steady stream of Blue Herons, ducks, lizards, butterflies, dragonflies, Osprey, hawks, beavers, toads, rattle snakes, scorpions and flies. Amazingly enough, no mosquitoes!

Perhaps the most optimistic of all were the Hall brothers—Badger, Wocnis and Strat. They each brought a fly swatter. In the middle of this great canyon with millions of flies, they sat on their boats or at the camp sites—swinging away and singing, "Die fly die; in the air everywhere, die fly die; In the sand, on my hand, die fly die; On my leg or on my egg, die fly die; Here and there, they're everywhere, die fly die; In a rut or on my butt, die fly die; On the oar, you little whore, die fly die; In your eye, don't ask why; die fly die."

"Now why would anyone want to swat flies in the great outdoors?" I asked.

"It's my way of getting back at them," Wocnis said as he hovered over an innocent baby fly with his Louisville Slugger fly swatter. "Die fly die!"

"SPLAT!"

A big grin spread across Wocnis' face.

We pitched camp that night on a beach sandbar above the rapid. Behind us, deep canyons cut through to, we knew not where.

Quickly, tents dotted the sandbar. Strat placed the 'Groover' in a private niche in the bushes. Everyone took a solar shower. We set up the kitchen. Food appeared! Brenda, Sally and Cindy—master chefs of the canyon, worked the kitchen like a violin.

But for me, a rock stood out in the river 100 meters away. Located near the first breaks of white water, it allowed a place for a chair. I grabbed mine, along with my notebook and headed along the shore.

The boulder set ten feet into the shallow water so I had to hop from rock to rock to get to it. Once there, I unfolded my chair and slid into the perfect grand-stand seat. In front of me, the slow liquid movement of the first rollers broke over the boulders in the middle of the river. White water raged to my left and the still waters of the Colorado from upstream headed toward me. High canyon walls narrowed a fading blue sky above. All around me, the sound of 'white river' music played on the hot breeze that tugged at my collar.

What does a person write while sitting on a rock in the middle of a river at the bottom of a 1.7 billion-year-old canyon? I thought about how wondrous this sight before me and that I could see it, feel it, hear it and touch it. I felt extreme gratitude, wonder and awe with my good fortune and that of my friends. How lucky to live this grand adventure—to travel through a billion years of nature's creative artistry. This Grand Canyon offered hundreds of wonders in its ancient walls. Above us, a mile up, the red sandstone cliffs framed the sky. The setting sun burned fiery red against the cliff faces. The cotton candy strawberry clouds slowly rushed across the sky as if pulled by "Chariots of Fire."

Robert Service said, "Have you gazed on naked grandeur where there's nothing else to gaze on, set pieces and drop-curtain scenes galore; big mountains heaved to heaven, which the blinding sunsets blazon; black canyons where the rapids rip and roar? Have you swept the visioned valley with the green stream streaking through it, searched the vastness for a something you have lost? Have you strung your soul to silence? Then for God's sake go and do it; hear the challenge, learn the lesson, pay the cost. Have you wandered in the wilderness, the sagebrush desolation; the bunch-grass levels where the cattle grazed? Have you whistled bits of rag-time at the end of all creation, and learned the desert's little ways? Have you camped upon the foothills, have you galloped o'er the ranges, have you roamed the arid sun-lands through and through? Have you chummed up with the mesa? Do you know its moods and changes? Listen to the wild—it's calling you!"

The drama above me vanished when the sun dropped below the horizon. Darkness closed in like a thief in the shadows. Not only that, the river rose from the Glen Canyon Dam dropping another 6,000 cubic feet per second into the river the day before. I needed to get out of there or I would be spending the night sleeping in my chair on a rock out in the river. I waded ashore and made my way back to camp.

Strat strummed his guitar and Wocnis mouthed his harmonica.

Brenda, Sally and Cindy cooked up a storm of salmon steaks. The men sat in chairs surrounding the kitchen while Gary baked a pie in his Dutch oven.

Overhead, the Big Dipper again fit into the space between the mountains and a billion stars sprinkled the sky with points of light. Far off in the darkness, the faint, yet glistening wings of the Dish Fairies made their appearance over the canyon walls.

Later, Rickiness, Steviness and Frostiness lowered their landing gear for a perfect entry into the dirty dishes of the kitchen. All slept well in the sanctuary of the Grand Canyon.

CHAPTER 8—The emerging creative energy of the universe

> *"How deep our sleep last night in the mountain's heart, beneath the trees and stars, hushed by solemn-sounding waterfalls and many small soothing voices in sweet accord whispering peace. Along the river, over the hills, in the ground, in the sky, spring work is going on with joyful enthusiasm, new life, new beauty, unfolding, unrolling in glorious exuberant extravagance, new birds in their nets, new winged creatures in the air, and new leaves , new flowers, spreading, shining, rejoicing everywhere."*
>
> John Muir

We grabbed a day of rest—to do nothing—relax and sit around. I awoke and returned to my rock to read. The river dropped. My rock no longer submerged in water. The sun readied itself to rise over the canyon rim. When it did, the river lit up and white water sparkled like diamonds. The canyon turned red/tan/gold/ black/brown in the many cliffs above me.

The sun lifted high into the sky from the eastern end of the canyon and burned hot on my cheeks and neck. We faced a scorcher of a day. I read and wrote until noon.

Gary came over and invited me to come up to the end of a small box canyon to spend the rest of the day in the shade and near a cooling waterfall. A 25-minute walk carried me out of the 103-degree heat.

A half-hour later, I packed up my chair, some food and headed up the canyon. Gravel and boulders served as my pathway up a dry riverbed. Millions of years of flash floods cut this small canyon. Great swaths of rock had been swept away by erosion.

I walked on until the canyon ended with a waterfall dropping a shower of water from a green plant, which had grown into the cliff face, 20 meters overhead. We walked into a horseshoe-shaped rock walled sitting room. Layers of sandstone created a multi-colored mosaic tapestry for our enjoyment. A red/tan rocky floor completed the room with a huge blue skylight above us. Everyone sat and read, or played chess and backgammon. I sat down and read Deepak Chopra's ***Seven Laws of Spiritual Fulfillment***. It dropped to a nice 80 degrees in the shade and the spray from the waterfall cooled the air even more.

During that five-hour stay, several people sat in the pool beneath the waterfall. When Sally came up, she rested on her back and stayed in the falls until she had cooled off. Wocnis hiked up for the fourth time and he too, relaxed in the pool.

By 5:30 in the afternoon, the day waned. Everyone packed up and walked back down to the main camp. I stayed behind to listen to the silence. It quieted my soul. I walked out at dusk.

As I walked along, Chopra's words played on my mind. This life is an adventure and it is a giving up of what is known to move into the unknown. It's like walking. We don't walk so much as we fall forward into the future. As we are about to fall on our faces, our other foot moves out to stop of us from falling. Yet, we keep falling and saving ourselves. When we do that, we give ourselves to uncertainty. It's scary and exciting at the same time.

Chopra's word echoed in my mind, "Relinquish your attachment to the known, step into the unknown, and you will step into the field of all possibilities. In your willingness to step into the unknown, you will have the wisdom of uncertainty factored in. This means that in every moment of your life, you will have excitement, adventure and mystery. You will experience the fun of life—the magic, the celebration, the exhilaration, and the exultation of your own spirit. Uncertainty is the fertile ground of creativity and freedom."

In so many ways, I've been accused of being too enthusiastic. A friend of mine, Pam, also possesses uncommon enthusiasm. Some people actually recoil from her energy. What they don't know is that her vibrancy equates to living energy. The root word for 'enthusiasm' is Latin for 'en Theo' which means: 'with God'. If God is the 'emerging creative energy of the universe', then, anyone with a great deal of 'enthusiasm' is continually moving with God or with the emerging creative energy. No wonder such people live 'enthusiastically'.

Would you rather be around a dull person or do you turn on to an enthusiastic person? Do you like the safety of the known or the unknown? Richard Bach, the creator of Jonathan Livingston Seagull, wrote in his ***Running from Safety***: "Why does growing up spiritually mean never growing up? Can we peacefully co-exist with the consequences of our choices? Why is it that only by running from safety can we make our wildest dreams take flight?"

I've been trying to figure that one out all my life. I'm going to keep trying. I'm going to keep my spirit alive by keeping my enthusiasm at full throttle.

One day, the answers most certainly will appear. If not, I'll keep trying. That's the adventure of living: "Many of life's failures are people who did not realize how close they were to success when they gave up."

As Winston Churchill, the famous Prime Minister of Great Britain said, "Never give in, never give in, never, never, never, never—in nothing, great or small, large or petty—never give in except to convictions of honor and good sense."

CHAPTER 9—Nothing! That's the beauty of it

> *"Energy can be a blessing. Like a river, it can bring life, but untamed it can unleash a raging flood of destruction. The body will do whatever it has to in order to bleed off excess energy. If it isn't spent consciously, in creative endeavors, physical activity, or sexual relations, then the subconscious will blow off energy, in fits of anger or cruelty, or nightmares, or crime, or illnesses, or through abuse of alcohol, tobacco, other drugs or food, or sex. Untamed energy, meeting internal obstacles, is the source of all addictions. Don't try to manage the addictions—clear the obstacles."*
> Dan Millman

Mile marker 125. We packed and left camp early. I nodded to my 'thinking rock' as we entered the rapid. Our one-day layover provided a good time for contemplation and resting our souls. When I think about it, how many people take time like that? In our society, everyday rushes helter-skelter in the city. We're surrounded by houses, power lines, whizzing cars, fast food joints and busy living. TV injects a cancer in every house. It mesmerizes us into buying things and watching the news, which rages bad day in and day out.

It occurred to me that we hadn't seen a slice of civilization in a week. We immersed ourselves in total wilderness. A few jet plane contrails over head broke that reality once in a while. Other than that, we only heard, felt, and touched wilderness.

Aldous Huxley, in ***Brave New World*** talked about his noble hero turning from his "Utopia" to the wilderness. He broke out of the 'perfection' and boredom of his protective bubble city to discover life struggles in the wilderness. "The savage is offered only two alternatives, an insane life in Utopia, or the life of a primitive in an Indian village."

In the recent movie, "Avatar" by James Cameron, he reproduced the mythical 'Eden' of planet Earth on another world named: "Pandora." The ten foot, skinny natives with large eyes lived in harmony with their environment. Up until 150 years ago, most of humanity lived in harmony with nature. But, with the development of the Industrial Revolution, automobiles, chemicals and plastics—humans stepped outside the "Circle of Life." The farther we separate ourselves from nature's rhythms, the more problematic our conditions on this planet. Avatar pointed it out clearly, but I don't think Americans and most 'modern' civilizations understand their own plight as humans degrade this planet on many different levels, i.e., species extinction, climate change, acidified oceans, water shortages and relentless pollution. I suspect nature will roar back, like the natives of Pandora, and crush modern civilizations to return them back to the basics.

As fossil fuels decline, our species faces an interesting if not degraded future on this planet.

I feel blessed that I can return to the wilderness via backpack or snowshoes or bicycle whenever I need to reconnect. When I think of all the people who have grown fat and placid in front of a TV in this country, it makes me wonder if our current day Utopia works. It seems that we humans in the modern world have stepped so far outside the "Circle of Life" that we lose our spiritual base. It's why so many are so lonely and going just a little bit crazy. That's not a judgment; just an observation. I may be as crazy as anyone.

As we floated, shadows kept us cool for most of the morning. We raced over many rapids through the narrows of the canyon. Crashing waves soaked me each time. The initial fright of the first few days had subsided and I looked forward to the big rollers and the wild ride through their watery rage.

Drifting along, we watched an army of barrel cacti seemingly looking down from behind every rock, much like the 'Kilroy' character.

One thing the river did not allow was 'hurriedness'. The river flowed not only slowly physically, but it allowed a person to be in perfect sync spiritually. Anyone who might be into a fast paced life would be forced to slow down on the river. From gridlock to oarlock! With gridlock, you can't wait to get moving and with oarlock, you're already home. One causes Excedrin numbing stress and the other, euphoric bliss. From "race and go" to slow and you're already "there." From a busy, cluttered life, to consummate simplicity!

"Keep pulling on those oars, Gary," I said, smiling.
"What's on your mind?" he asked.
"Nothing," I said. "That's the beauty of it."

River life makes me realize how noisy and overwhelming our lives are in this modern America. We're being pushed beyond our natural capacity, our natural cycles. For all the conveniences of our computers and microwave ovens, we're being pulled too fast to do too much. Those that 'power up' gain success and a lot of stuff. The rest gain stress and spiritual poverty. It eats at their inner beings.

But on the river, basic living brings basic happiness. Food, water, sleep, rowing, friendships and simple conversation! Although, we have gotten into a couple of heated talks on politics! We mostly talk about hikes, bikes, and outdoor adventure. Rick talked about a snow climb he once took where one of his partners fell off the edge and was saved by being roped in. Steve talked about his backpacking trips along the Colorado Trail. Badger talked about raft trips down the Middle Fork River. Strat talked in the songs he wrote. Brenda shared stories from Africa and South America.

My friend John Muir said, "No healthy man who delivers himself into the hands of nature can possibly doubt the doubleness of his life. Soul and body receive separate nourishment and separate exercise, and speedily reach a stage of development wherein each is easily known apart from the other. Living artificially in town, we are sickly, and never come to know ourselves. Our torpid souls are hopelessly entangled with our torpid bodies, and not only is there a confused mingling of our own souls with our own bodies, but we hardly possess a separate existence from our neighbors."

Today, I think the key is to 'know' what modern living does to one's spiritual self and attempt to 'reharmonize' with nature by returning to her woods, streams and wildness whenever possible.

The canyon narrowed again—bringing giant burps of black, polished lava into view that looked as shiny as new bowling balls. Inside the lava, more fissures of quartz rock created intricate designs. So much geology presented itself that I didn't understand. I vowed to take a class when I returned home.

Along this stretch, several tiers of the canyon revealed themselves. The primary walls of 2,000 feet sometimes cracked and gave way to secondary cliffs over 4,000 feet high. The sun shone through the V-shaped valleys like a giant spotlight blazing through a nightclub and lighting up the main entertainer.

The barrel cacti, round, three feet tall and with bulbous heads seemed like an army that watched our every move. They grew behind every rock along the canyon. We found it intriguing that they grew in over 120-degree summer heat. Even more astounding: they grew on black lava rock. That meant they lived in temperatures approaching 180 or more degrees F. Their roots fried 12 hours a day and any water they might have reached, evaporated instantly. Still, they grew strong and green.

Life finds a way. It possesses a will. It engages a method. Why else would it begin and thrive out here on this lone planet in this vast galaxy in the middle of the universe. Did I say middle? Heck we could be in a tiny corner of the universe for all we know. Can we find the answer of where we are or 'why' we are in the universe?

Probably not, but we can have fun trying. The only danger in the quest is the unsettling debunking of the myths and traditions our culture drilled into us. It's hard to cut through the religions, legends and voodoo of the past. Nonetheless, the show goes on—with or without us.

In the morning, we arrived at the 'Doll House' just before Head Rock Rapid. The Doll House featured a purple/black rock about one story high that had been carved by erosion into many chambers. We stopped and climbed around, through, up and down its many rooms. Once again, nature provided us with yet another mystery and play moment.

We pulled into the river after having worn ourselves out in the Doll House. Head Rock Rapid proved a challenge for Wocnis. A massive rock the size of a two-bedroom house rose smack dab in the middle of the river. To the left, raging water poured into a funnel that we couldn't see from the other side. To the right, it slid down over shallow rocks, but to get to it we had to first pass a large rock on 'river right' which carried us into the current that would force us left. Only a strong pull on the oars would move us to the right and on to the 'known' safer ride.

Wocnis didn't make it and got boiled over to the eddy on the left near a treacherous rock wall. From there, the current spun him around like a CD disk. His only choice: the 'chute' of angry, seething, howling danger ahead of him.

As Gary maneuvered our raft into position, I saw Wocnis grip the oars and bust his butt with all his might. His 'Cataract' raft bolted out of the eddy and barged into the violent white water. From there, he swung his nose hard to the right and vanished behind Head Rock.

At the same time, Gary had his own challenge to deal with as he passed the big rock on 'river right' but was sucked into the left white water current. He ripped on the oars twice before our 'River Slug' pulled out of the main current. Slowly, it moved away and slid through the roiling rapids to the right.

Once caught in the secondary current, we moved by the large rock and funneled back into the main stream. Badger floated in front and just as we turned around, Wocnis floated free and upright below us. He made it. WHAT a story he would have at the campfire tonight.

Again, we drifted until we passed Christmas Cave. A large cavern, big enough for several single engine planes, imploded into the rock wall about 50 feet above the water. Gary and I cruised past. The current slowed. We drifted. I worked the oars while Gary wrote in his journal. Bumping along that narrow canyon felt like rowing alongside an aircraft carrier. The walls rose straight up from the water.

Early in the afternoon, I looked up from my oars to see a deep blue with white spray, eight-foot wide waterfall shooting down out of a red stone wall. It looked like someone had built a 100 foot high shower out of the rock. The water fell back into the rocks and into a brilliant crystal blue pool. I had never seen anything like it. We gazed upon Deer Creek Falls.

We pitched camp on the opposite side on a high sandbar. Unfortunately, the wind blew into our faces and sandblasted us enough to where we had to go down to the rafts to read, write and relax.

Gary unloaded our raft and found a scorpion. When darkness descended upon us, mice and scorpions crawled into our wilderness kitchen. We faced an invasion. The mice raced around the rocks, across the sand and between our legs. One bold scorpion marched up to a mouse to dispute a piece of tofu that had fallen off the table. One thing about scorpions, they 'led' with their stingers, which was attached to their tails, which curled back over their heads. One hit from that toxic tail could send anyone to the hospital. But out there, you'd have to survive on your own.

I talked to Badger who explained his heart attack in detail and the operation that opened up his arteries. He spoke so matter of fact about living and dying. But, he preferred living.

Brenda, Cindy and Sally again cooked up a fabulous meal with carrot cake for dessert. Rick and I took over the dishwashing.

Quickly, everyone retired to his or her raft or tent for a good night's sleep. As was my custom, I didn't put my tent up until the last minute so I would not have mice chewing holes through it trying to find food. It happened once in Joshua Tree National Park and my new tent suffered holes in the floor. I haven't made 'that' mistake again.

After pitching the tent, I left the rain fly off to keep cool during the night. I hadn't gotten into my sleeping bag the whole trip because of the heat. Besides, I could watch the stars through my skylight netting.

Later that night, I slept away when a fierce wind blew in from the west. I felt the tent shift with a few blasts across my port bow, but quickly faded into sleep. Thereafter, the wind pummeled my tent mercilessly for the next two hours. For some reason, I woke up with sand on my lips and in my mouth. I ran my hand over my belly and felt a thin layer of sand. Sand crystals dusted my ears and piled up in the corners of my eyes. I turned over on my bag to notice sand had crept its way onto my sleeping bag and more of it had piled onto my pillow. It so disturbed me that I reached for my miner's lamp and turned it on.

"Ye gods!" I muttered.

My tent looked like a sandbox. So many particles had blown through the netting that a fine layer of red sand covered everything. It settled in my ears, nose, hair and on my skin. I felt the grit between my teeth. About one-eighth inch of sand covered the bottom of my tent.

I couldn't do anything about it so I dusted off my pillow, turned on my side and fell back to sleep.

Where's that five star hotel that I've ranted against?

CHAPTER 10—Is it possible to get fat on nature's visions?

> *"One is constantly reminded of the infinite lavishness and fertility of nature—inexhaustible abundance amid what seems enormous waste. And yet when we look into any of her operations that lie within reach of our minds, we learn that no particle of her material is wasted or worn out. It is eternally flowing from use to use, beauty to yet higher beauty."*
>
> John Muir

We ate cold cereal, packed up and headed across the river to Deer Creek Falls the next morning.

Rock cliffs confined the falls, so much so, that it looked like water flowed through a huge test tube about five feet in diameter. But when it hit 100 feet below—into a deep blue pool—it sent out a white spray that created a cool breeze even on the hottest day.

Steve, Rick and I, alias, the Grand Canyon Dish Fairies, grabbed our water bottles and cameras, and headed up a rocky trail to the source of the falls. We labored over Cadillac-sized boulders until we reached a trail that switch-backed up to the left side of the falls. Up we climbed through pinion bushes, Fishhook cactus and brush. We climbed through a world of horrid heat, layered rock and dusty terrain. At 300 feet above the river, the morning sun created a gauzy haze over the canyon.

The Colorado River shimmered in a dream-like state with several other rafts floating through the mist. At 400 feet, we reached solid rock that led back into a narrow crevasse. We walked along a trail that hugged the cliffs. Below us, the river cut ribbon-like waves into the rocks for millions of years. We heard the water, but couldn't see it because it was hidden by the waving action of the rocks and many layers that protruded outward.

The trail hugged tightly to the wall and one slip would drop a person a hundred feet in seconds. The trail undulated along the wall much like a child's snaking race car track. Further along, the river appeared again. It ran wild through twists and turns in the rock floor.

Still further we hiked in until the river drew closer and closer to the trail. The polished rock smoothed into a playground slide where the river continued cutting its path. Presto! The creek that fed the falls raced under our feet and fell from yet another falls near a band of trees 50 yards further back. Behind the falls, the desert spread back to high canyon walls. The waterfall dropped into a small pool that drained into the rock bed. I jumped in and took a cooling shower.

The trip back dropped us down to the bottom of the falls where the spray rushed horizontally across the pool.

Upon seeing the same sight 141 years ago, Powell wrote: "Just after dinner, we passed a stream on the right, which leaped into the Colorado by a direct fall of more than 100 feet, forming a beautiful cascade. On the rocks in the cave-like chamber are ferns, with delicate fronds and enameled stalks."

Here it is a century later and the same falls has been cascading down this rock face with the ancestors of the same plants delighting our eyes and spirits. What Powell saw, we enjoyed, too. What he wrote about, I too, write my story.

Isn't that the wonder of being alive? Each of us explores this world in whatever ways available in our lives. In a free country, any of us may become whatever it is that burns with passion inside our hearts. Gary has become a fantastic dancer in the middle of his life. Wocnis creates art and plays the guitar. Strat writes songs that he shares with all of us. To me, he's James Taylor all over again. Brenda works as a social activist on the environmental front. Steve hikes the Colorado Trail. Julie teaches kids to skate. Badger expounds on wisdom. Ivan works toward his Alpaca farm. Rick and Cindy take adventures around the world. Sally educates on the environment. All of us follow our hearts and passions. Like Powell, I am blessed to be able to write about my adventures. We enjoy good fortune to live our lives while expressing our passions.

After pumping three seven-gallon containers full of filtered water, we shoved the boats into the middle of the river. The day proceeded and our flotilla of winged river birds glided down the Colorado. Gary dug his 'wings' into the water as we surged down the glassy tongue of Deer Creek Rapid. That familiar rush of water sucked us down and pulled us into the wildest ride of the day.

We oared without incident until we arrived at Matkatamiba. We pulled 'river left' into a beige-colored canyon just before a rapid. After tying up the boats, we entered a very narrow walkway, almost tunnel-like, and ate lunch on some gray rock ledges. A small creek about one foot across and six inches deep rushed downward past us.

While we stood around eating lunch, a small bat crawled along the canyon wall. It suffered an injury and couldn't fly, but it pulled itself toward a corner of the rocks. Once there, it placed its wings over its head and rested.

"Poor thing," Cindy said.

"It's probably going to be scorpion dinner tonight," Steve said.

The cruel truth was that the bat would most likely die because it was unable to fly. It didn't know it, but it was on its deathbed. There was nothing any of us could do. We left it alone.

We walked into the canyon after lunch.

Strat, who had rafted the canyon before, said, "This little piece of God's handiwork probably took millions of years, but it's one of His best."

"Lead on," I said.

The creek cut through thousands of layers sedimentary rock. We walked through a cut of what could pass for the world's largest stack of pancakes. Some layers were thin cakes and others thick. All featured sand and rock between them. We noted that one day; all our bodies would be part of some geological rock layer a million years into the future.

Walking up, the clear stream moved from flowing over gravel into flowing over solid rock. Above, 1,000-foot canyon walls dwarfed us. Tiny cacti grew from the layers.

While stopping to take pictures, the group left me behind. I followed the creek until I turned a corner where a five-foot waterfall fell over green/black rock with four Japanese rice paddy terraces that caused the water to tumble to the bottom. Red stone cut inlays through the green that was enhanced by the water. Right after the falls, the little canyon wound like a ribbon in the wind on both sides into a blended mirage—as if I looked into one of those funny mirrors at a carnival.

I followed the water over smoothly polished rock to another waterfall that snaked down from ten feet and fell into a five-foot wide pool and a foot deep. I climbed still further until the creek vanished into a rock narrow less than two feet wide. It felt like being in a cave. I followed upward. Then I saw the creek again racing toward me and downward like a roller coaster. Up I climbed. A large boulder that had crashed into the creek had stopped the wild ride of the water. No matter. The water backed up and then raced past the rock with another waterfall.

Past the tiny dam, the water once again spiraled through the rock like a runaway roller-coaster.

"Good grief! Nature is astonishingly creative," I muttered to myself.

I traveled up this marvelous winding mystery tour until yet another waterfall. After climbing it, I followed the creek through more cuts through the pancake layers until it rushed out of a dead end canyon amphitheater. I walked into a natural kiva with ferns, trees, flowers and bushes set in an almost elegant living room that you might see on "The Rich and Famous."

The creek rushed out over flat rock and formed three pools before knifing through the rock again on its journey downward. A few large boulders stood in indolent elegance after having fallen from far above. All around me—red, tan, brown, gray rock painted the kiva in earth-tone contrasts.

Around the amphitheater, the pancake layers formed stadium seating for anyone who wanted to watch the magic show before them.

Above us, a slender, roughly lined sliver of blue sky with swallows flying across it became our ceiling. I sat down on the bleachers wondering who wrote the master plan for this amazing piece of landscape architecture. No human could have achieved it—because it took several billions of years and the work continues.

We hiked up the canyon where it once again widened and astounded our eyes. The sheer rock cliffs rose 2,000 feet above us where red rocks collided with blue sky. The stream flowed over rocks and sand on its way to the Colorado.

The group left me again as I took more pictures and tried to capture the beauty in my mind. I walked back down into the kiva where the pools of water flowed into each other and polished the rock like a rich man's granite kitchen counter top. I sat on the rock bleachers. As I sat there, I could not have imagined that a tiny stream could cut such a mighty and extravagantly gorgeous canyon into an amazing piece of paradise. Sure, flash floods added their mark, with winter freezing and erosion from the rain—but it was the stream that cut, inch by inch, century after century, millennia upon millennia—into the rock that formed the canyon that formed the pools and the place where I sat. I settled back to gaze upon my surroundings and felt simply—humble.

Gary awaited me at the boat. The rest of the group had gone. I felt rich from sensory overload.

"Let's go," he said.

"This trip is the greatest gift you've ever given me," I said. "I couldn't thank you enough in a hundred years."

Gary smiled.

Later that evening, I found a point on the river away from everyone. Sitting there under the star spangled canopy of the universe, I pondered if it was possible to get enough of this kind of wonder? Could I over-load, over-eat, over-indulge nature's banquet? Is it possible to get fat on nature's visions? Could I over-do myself?

If it's possible, I will have done just that on this 16-day journey on this great river through time.

CHAPTER 11—Go through our lives without noticing our lives

> *"You are what your deep, driving desire is.*
> *As your desire is, so is your will.*
> *As your will is, so is your deed.*
> *As your deed is, so is your destiny."*
>   Upanishad

Gary pulled hard on the oars to get us out into the rapid and away from the rock cliffs that shot vertically out of the river. He oared along while I wrote notes on the artwork in the canyon. The river made a few curls left and right until it turned around a bend where the roar deafened the air around us.

"My God, those waves are HUGE!" I said.

"Could get wet," Gary said.

"Hell, we could get more than wet," I said. "What's the name of this rapid?"

"Upset!"

"No kidding," I said and prepared myself by putting my notes in plastic and checked my camera for waterproofing.

Gary stood up to survey the rapid. We floated 50 yards from the tongue. I stood up, too. BIG! Rock fangs and grizzly-like claws tore upward from under the water. Less than 100 feet into the rapid, the water smashed into a rock wall and tumbled savagely to the right. Gary would have to pull hard right to miss the waves coming in that could flip us.

Then came the quiet of the maw and the glassy tongue of the stillness of the approach and I sat on the bench with my hands clutched on the straps. The first roller heaved ten feet skyward. Only one way to get past it: over the top—where Gary headed.

Down, down and still further down the raft dropped as if headed into the deepest chambers of hell. As soon as we could go no further the boat rolled upward on its way to the crest of the wave. We smashed over the top with 20 gallons of water pouring into the raft. (Think I'm kidding? Look at the cover of the book!) The next roller suffered a side-cut by the force of the water being pushed back off the rock cliffs about ten feet to our left. We got sucked into the hole and I only looked on helplessly as the next waved showed the face of an angry ax murderer who had found his next victim.

Me!

Gary followed, but he furiously pulled right because we faced the treachery of the rock wall only 50 feet in front of us. When we hit the peak, the water smashed us again and threw me backward with my legs flying upward. I fell left then nearly tossed violently right when the raft reacted to the wall of water.

Gary reefed on the oars. The 'River Slug' pulled away as we neared the deadly cliffs. The rollers diminished to six feet, then five, then four.

"That was the best ride on the river so far," I yelled.

"Doesn't compare to Lava Falls," Gary said.

"It doesn't?" I murmured.

"You'll see," he said.

What kind of death trap would be Lava Falls? From listening to the Hall brothers, it seemed that Lava provided the mythical rapid that undid many a boatman, even the notorious river outlaw "High Water Harry" was terrified of Lava Falls according to Wocnis.

The rest of the group had watched the drama and once all of us passed safely through the falls, they headed to Ledges Campground. Like its name, we camped on ledges composed of layered rock projecting into the river. We stepped up on the rocks to secure the boats. Long lines from the boats tied to boulders above us. In back of the camp, the cliffs soared upward into a great amphitheater 3,500 feet above our heads.

After unpacking, I decided to swim across the river.

"It's about this time in the trip that people start doing strange things," Gary said of my swim. "You have to wear a life preserver."

"Okay."

I donned the orange vest and a wet suit top. I walked up river and dove in. I pulled hard against the downward current. I quickly made the other side—touched the wall—and swam back with plenty of time to reach Gary's boat.

"Piece of cake," I said.

Lasagna and vegetables along with garlic bread brought out the best of everyone that night. Brenda, Sally and Cindy continued cooking fantastic meals every evening. We men need women to spruce up our lives. If I rafted by myself on this trip, I'd eat potato soup with lentils out of a can or cooked rice out of a box every night for a month. My breakfast would be oatmeal and raisins. I'd look like a grubby old gold miner in no time. The more I get into the wilderness, the more I LOOK like wilderness. The women want a hot shower each night and get it with the new solar heated plastic bags that cook in the sun all day. But me? Hell, I love freezing my ass off taking a bath in the frigid waters of the river.

I've been asked that many times, "Why would you jump into a freezing river instead of enjoying a hot shower?"

Most of us in the USA are so comfortable most of the time that we go through our lives without noticing our lives. On an adventure, I love the sensations of life more than the comforts of life. I can always enjoy a hot shower at home. Who needs one in the wilderness? Why bring the comforts of home living into wilderness living? We might as well bring air conditioning, a flush toilet, microwave and a refrigerator on all our adventures. NOT ME! Give me some raw, unredeemed wilderness kick-ass living next to the very heartbeat of nature.

After dinner, Cindy called for the Dish Fairies to do the dishes. From that point on, Rick, Steve and I got a little caught up in being the 'masculine' side of a dish fairy. One joke after another ensued until we laughed hysterically.

That night, I headed for Gary's boat to sleep. I placed my air mattress on the back bench and rolled out my sleeping bag. Gary curled into his bedroll and listened to music from headphones as he stared up to the heavens.

"Don't mind me," he said. "I'm listening to my music."

That told me he wasn't in the mood for talking. We had done and seen so much that day that silence made a better companion along with the dark sky overhead.

I stuffed myself into my bag and dropped back on the floatation pad for a pillow. I peered into the ink black of space. Stars looked like raindrops in the sky—touched by silver light. Rolling my eyes left and right—black canyon walls enclosed the heavens as if I rested in the middle of an ancient city. I felt the gentle rocking of the raft as the river curled and swirled past us.

As I looked up to the sky, a simple feeling of being totally relaxed warmed my body. The night air remained still. My attention locked on the stars. They always inhabited the heavens but couldn't be seen except in the darkness of night. I gazed across the universe with no thoughts coming out of my head.

A white-hot light sliced across the sky.

"Meteor," I muttered.

Moments later, like the meteor, I too, vanished into the night.

About 2 a.m., I awoke when Wocnis, who slept on his boat next to Gary's, started yelling, "Get out of here!"

Startled, I sat up. A dozen mice had invaded Wocnis' boat by scampering up his mooring lines. They had sniffed and searched their way to some trail mix he had left out near his head. One had jumped across his arm and ran over his sleeping bag. Like a Hitchcock movie, they swarmed all over him. From there, with Wocnis flailing and yelling, the mice abandoned ship.

I dropped back and looked up to the sky. My eyes quickly closed and I returned to never, never land.

At least the mice didn't have to do dishes!

CHAPTER 12—And miss the biggest orgasm of the trip?

> *"There is a pleasure in the pathless woods, there is a rapture on the lonely shore, there is society, where none intrudes, by the deep sea, music in its roar: I love not man the less, but Nature more."*
>
> Lord Byron

Behind our campsite, a gargantuan cirque framed in fire-engine red with a Thanksgiving white turkey meat colored middle—resembled a mosaic from grandma's finest quilt. Everyone sat talking in the kitchen area at breakfast, with no thoughts to getting on the river early. I decided to climb to that cirque. It rose 2,000 feet over the river. High vertical cliffs blocked my way as I sidestepped up the mountain.

Cactus, rocks and bushes made my climb more difficult because it was easy to slip. I watched every footfall. One slip into a barrel cactus and I would be pulling needles out of my legs and hands for hours. Another slip off the rock scree could cause a rock avalanche.

At 500 feet, I reached a black frozen molten lava formation featuring razor sharp edges. Interestingly enough, it was as if someone had mixed up a cake batter with M&M's, jelly beans and pennies—and poured it down the mountain. When it hardened, it created a nasty coral reef. Deadly to touch! Luckily, my shoes took all the pain and I did not complain.

At 1,000 feet, I worked my way into a cathedral of stone blocks, and by cautiously, like a cat walking through a dog kennel, working my way around them, I found a passage. It gave me some fright, as it climbed vertically. Once past that, I pulled again to the right and climbed still further where only broken rock awaited me.

"Good God, don't start a landslide," I said to myself. "My friends wouldn't stand a chance if the whole mountain came down on them."

At 1,500 feet, I glanced back. The river looked green and still. The boats looked like tiny dots on the water. I enjoyed an eagle's view. I turned up through a broken ledge and under an escarpment. From there, I delicately leaned into the cliff and cat walked along a six inch narrow ledge of rock. Below me was 500 feet of air. If I slipped, I would need to grow wings quickly or call the morgue for a reservation.

The mountain gods spared me and I made my way across. Another few minutes and I found myself on a ledge at the far-left side of the rock fortress I had been climbing. Before me, I saw a vast tan/red sandstone cirque a halfmile across and a half-mile high. I stood at the ground floor as it soared upward into the morning sky. It exploded in colors with the rising sun. The red rock framed it like a picture and the white middle came close to looking like the "Bull's eye" for an archery target. Above it all, azure sky! I felt like a tiny mouse in a great kingdom of rocks.

The trip down moved quickly until I tried to scoot down a V-wedge slot, but sat on a cactus. Needles made a pin cushion out of my butt in an instant.

"DAMN!" I yelled.

It took me 20 minutes to pull the needles out of, first, my pants, and then my swim trunks underneath, and finally the ones that pierced my skin.

As I stood there 800 feet above the river, I remembered Dan Millman's book, ***No Ordinary Moments***. Here I sat on top of a cliff having a cactus needle-in-my-ass moment while my friends sat around the comfort of the breakfast table sipping coffee.

No matter; each precious moment entails another and another until they create the mosaic of our lives. The threads that weave the brilliant, sometimes sober tapestry we each live came from days weaving into weeks, months and years. Even my new friends, each enjoyed a personal story of triumph and tragedy. Marriage, divorce, kids gone away, dreams not realized, et al. Even the successful ones experienced their troubles, too. One had suffered a heart attack and walked a tight rope between life and death. Even at that, it's been good to get this old to even have a chance for a heart attack. Many don't make it past their youth.

So, I'm having a cactus needle-in-my-ass moment—and what a thrill it is! Thank you Great Spirit for the little things. They mean so much!

We eased into the river late in the morning. Mile marker 150! The sun shone on the canyon walls the color of sliced ham on brown rye bread. Thin streaks of black 'desert varnish' swept down the rocks like quiet dark waterfalls.

Several big horned sheep gazed indolently at us as we passed them. A blue heron took flight when we came too close. Several yellow and black winged butterflies played on the air currents above our raft. On the high cliffs, ocotillo trees, with long slender green branches enjoyed backlighting from the sun. They looked like upside down jellyfish with their green tentacles extending into the air.

Gary maneuvered the 'River Slug' through a half dozen rapids before we stopped at the Havasu River junction.

For those who don't know the magic of this little known canyon, it is a paradox-paradise of water and desert deep within the Grand Canyon. About nine miles from the southwest rim of the canyon and nine miles from the Colorado River, the Havasu River begins as a clear turquoise spring boiling out of the desert sand. From such unlikely beginnings, the water flows 18 miles through the Havasupai (canyon of the blue green waters) and creates a paradise of waterfalls and exotic pools. A calcium like substance known as 'travertine' gets picked up by the water and builds dams, pools and waterfalls on its journey down a desolate desert canyon. Twenty feet on either side of the brilliant turquoise water Mother Nature created a Garden of Eden full of flowers, fauna, trees, butterflies, birds, bats and fish. Outside that line you find a scorching desert where only cactus and lizards thrive in the deadly heat.

We moored the boats.

I climbed a series of rock ledges and made my way into the canyon. Below, the Havasu River cut through 50 feet of solid gray rock. It left magical catacombs of smooth rock and a brilliant turquoise "River of Styx." Beyond, and higher into the canyon, sparkling water crashed through assorted boulders and pools created by the travertine. Above me, 2,000-foot sandstone canyon walls created a mystic tunnel through that paradise.

After crossing the river dozens of times and being caught up in boiling white water bubbles in the pools created by the calcium-like travertine, I arrived at one of the most amazing sights in the world. On either side of the stream, life flourished. But outside 20 feet along the stream, the desert and lizards dominated. So, there, in front of me, like a Disney dream world movie, dropped a 130-foot waterfall of crystal deep blue water and white spray. Mooney Falls fell into a dream-like pool of water with brown leafy fern-like rocks surrounding it that created a vase-effect all the way to the top. Over the centuries, the travertine had built up and forced the falls to wave back and forth across the canyon like a windshield wiper. In its path, the water left drooping fern-shaped leaves cascading downwards in a half circle. And so, there I stood with blue sky above…white spray crashing across the pool…a gushing blue waterfall erupting from the crack in the rocks at the top of the rim and garnished with lush green plants on either side of the water. Added to that, the white music of the rushing water carried across the canyon. If this was a fantasy, my friends and I lived it.

What do you do when you're living in the middle of a fantasy? That's easy! You jump in with no clothes on!

For anyone lucky enough to explore this "Eden" on Earth, it's beyond breathtaking and spiritually astounding.

Back at the Colorado River, Gary oared for the rest of the day. That left me time to read and write—as well as gaze in profound and continued astonishment at the immense rock walls soaring above us on both sides of the river. Every kind of formation greeted us along the way. The cliffs, always red, brown and tan—cut jagged angles, squares, oblongs, tubes, spires, triangles and arrows into the rocks. Somewhere in its billion years of cutting the canyon, the Colorado River etched out the most exotic creations including church cathedrals, spires, Gothic columns, Roman coliseums, arching bridges, enormous caves, amphitheaters, soaring skyscrapers and elegant stone statues representing something the universe needed to create.

I sat there in the raft in the middle of ALL that mind-bending creation, and felt immeasurably humble. My 'wonder' circuits exploded. My eyes, like vacuum cleaners, sucked it all into my mind. My spirit soared on the cliffs like the hawk I watched sailing the thermals. For all I knew, I might be the hawk. What's the difference?

Endless natural wonders greeted us daily to become ho-hum. But, they didn't allow such an attitude. This place commands your attention all the time. They, the rock cliffs, reach toward the heavens, while remaining still, while far below, the river, always moving—keeps etching away while the agitated wind cuts magic into the rock and the sun melts while the cold freezes.

What took billions of years and layers to form, took billions of years of cutting to arrive at this mind-boggling creation.

As Brenda said, "The Great Spirit made this for your enjoyment."

In the late afternoon, we men tied three rafts together and talked about women, football and women. Guy talk! It's about everything and nothing. Call it male bonding or what have you; it's a lot of fun bullshitting. We laughed, scratched and drank a few beers. Wocnis and Strat swatted a few flies. "Die fly, die!"

We camped at Nationals with a wild wind blowing. Brenda cooked a hot beef stroganoff and three-bean dinner. Gary baked a blue berry pie. The chairs circled the kitchen and the 'river talk' commenced.

Badger talked about a kayaker who had arrogantly shoved a guy's raft into the rapid at a takeout and spent 1.5 days chasing it down river, pulling it back up river and getting it back out. His one act of rudeness nearly cost another rafter his life and really pissed off a few people.

Wocnis related his own story about living through the raging water of House Rock Rapid.

Rick, a man of impeccable humor and unrepressed spirit—talked of his adventures on climbing Mount Rainier where, when he got to the top on a sunlit cloudless day, he saw all the way to forever. He also climbed Kilimanjaro and rafted the Zambezi.

Finally, Cindy decided to walk Lava Falls Rapid because of its treachery and terrifying holes that flipped the best of boats.

"Maybe I should walk Lava Falls, too," I said, sympathizing with Cindy.

"What?" Badger said. "And miss the biggest orgasm of the trip?"

"Guess I do Lava," I said.

"Friggin' A, you will," Steve said.

"It's settled," I said. "I'm doing Lava."

CHAPTER 13—Unholy, raging and terrifying stretch of water

> *"Some of the days I have spent alone in the depths of the wilderness have shown me that immortal life beyond the grave is not essential for perfect happiness."*
>
> John Muir

Dawn broke with a cool breeze over our camp. The sun, never visible for hours into the morning, lit up the high rock towers above us. A few yards from my tent on the beach, the waves slapped at the boats lined up and roped together. I'm sitting here thinking about the thrill of Lava Falls.

The BIG ONE! The one to give the most excitement and the most danger! God, we humans are so capricious! We demand security, safety and then, we run out into the wilderness and seek danger—seek ways of testing, yes, even killing ourselves. Every weekend around the country, men and women run out to hang from thin ropes on vertical cliffs. They fall and break their bones or heads, and some die. Others mount bucking Brahma bulls that gore and stomp them to death. Motorcyclists jump, race and crash into each other like ping pong balls in a lottery. Others bungee jump and sometimes, the cord breaks and they cease to exist. Some jump out of planes riding a snowboard! While I was in Antarctica, three guys jumped out of a plane over the South Pole. They hit the 70 below zero numbing wind at 18,000 feet above the Pole. It was like having a quart of ice cream shoved up their nostrils in seconds. They would have been the first to do it, but they didn't open their chutes (possibly because the ground was aspirin white and they couldn't visually judge when to pull the ripcords), and were the first to die doing it. One man jumped off a 90-foot cliff into a lake and broke his back, which caused him to be wheelchair bound for the rest of his life. One man jumped off a Seattle skyscraper, but his chute didn't open and he somehow crashed into an office window. Cuts and blood covered his body. Can you imagine you're a secretary typing away and some wild-man bursts through your office window on the 50th floor?! Dozens of other examples make the news weekly.

What drives such men to do such daredevil stunts? Are they crazy? What do they get out of them? Who are they?

A friend of mine was best friends with Steve Mulholland, one of the parachutists who skydived over the South Pole and died in 1998. After he died, Steve's friend wrote, "Steve and I met on a kayaking trip in Utah in the early 80s and from then on did lots of exciting and adventurous things. Do you know that he was the first and only person to ever BASE jump in Antarctica? He had intentions to be the first person to base jump on all of the seven continents, sort of like Dick Bass' Seven Summits trips. Steve was there for me at my wedding, helped me prepare my son's nursery, helped make my wife go into labor by walking her in adverse weather. He was there for the birth of my son. He had been on raft trips on the Selway at flood stage, a more terrifying experience than the Grand Canyon, any day! He knew many of my adventure friends. He was a 5.13+ climber who was the first person to ever put two of my friends at the end of a climbing rope on a Yampa raft trip. Steve followed the Grateful Dead around the country sometimes. He was weird Uncle Steve to my kids and always had a bed in my home. I attended his funeral in Indiana at the church where his mom was the minister. I toasted him with Jager Meister then, and on river trips with more of his friends as we mourned his passing.

"Having said all of this, Steve did deploy his chute belatedly, but not soon enough to prevent his death. I have talked to the surviving fourth member of the jump and with Steve's brothers at length trying to understand what happened, and nobody still knows or will ever know more than theories or guess work why this tragedy occurred. I think about Steve a lot. You and he would have instantly understood each other and known why you have chosen the paths that you have."

That's from a friend who loved a man who lived life at the edge. That's the glory of this amazing life adventure. Each of us gets to live it as he or she wishes. Many, and yes, I say, MANY sit on their butts their whole lives and squander decades by watching TV or being glued to a computer screen, find absolute meaning in NFL games, or they overeat, get fat and lazy—living their lives in a stupor. But that's what they get to choose because it's their lives—not yours, not mine, not anyone's. It's theirs to live as they wish. The key is that we all respect each other's choices. I respect the ones in front of the boob tube. I don't hang out with them, but I respect them.

How about the man who jumped off the cliff and broke his back? He suffered paralysis from the waist down. I know him. His name is Matt Feeney. God gave him glorious good looks and a body that women drooled over. He possesses charisma and power in his being that most politicians would give their first born to have. After breaking his back, Matt didn't sit on his butt and die of depression. Nor did he feel sorry for himself. He got back up from the bed and jumped into a wheelchair—in fact, started racing in wheel chairs. Later, he learned to race on a 'mono' ski. Still later, he bicycle raced (using his hands to pedal) and water skied at the Special Olympics. He formerly supervised and taught at the National Sports Center for the Disabled in Winter Park, Colorado. Today, he runs his own 'adaptive skiing' sports camps for the disabled. He's the kind of man and athlete that thousands of people look up to for guidance, power and inspiration. Even as he sits in that wheel chair, he tackles life everyday—with power, gusto, passion and purpose. It is my honor and privilege to be his friend. He has no idea how much I admire him, his courage and his actions as he leaps toward life.

Fact is, Steve Mulholland and Matt Feeney, and others like them represent our warriors. They don't sit around talking about doing great things. They DO them! Some like Reinhold Messner, the man who has summited Everest twice without oxygen and was the first to climb all 8,000 meter peaks—are smart, strong, cunning—AND lucky! Messner's brother equaled his talents, but on one climb, the brother walked five meters behind Reinhold when a crevasse gobbled him 1,000 feet down into an icy grave. Reinhold enjoyed the glory and his brother suffered an early exit.

But then, I ask, did his brother suffer? Fact is, like Jack London said, "I'd rather be a blazing meteor across the sky than a comfortable sleepy planet. Better to live my days than to extend them without passion or meaning."

That's what I call the 'Voluptuousness of Living." You charge into the teeth of life and you gulp, grab, wrestle, sing, scream and jump off a cliff or ride a bike across a continent. You make it a point to live each day with a sense of power and glory.

Guys like Steve Mulholland, Matt Feeney, Pasquale Scaturro, Shackleton, Lief Erikson, Daniel Boone, Chief Crazy Horse, Alexander the Great, Gandhi, Muir, Twain, Abbey and women like Susan B. Anthony, Wilma Rudolph, Fonda, Hillary Clinton, Babe Deitrickson, Lindsey Vonn, Julie Mancuso, Eleanor Roosevelt, Barbara Jordan, Oprah and many others are warriors. They paid a price and they live or lived their lives with passion. I honor them and their courage. They moved toward life and took chances. They pressed into the unknown so the rest of us might find the courage to try. They perspired and inspired. Their legacies allow each one of us more courage than we might otherwise have mustered. Steve Mulholland didn't just jump out of an airplane to his death. He jumped toward life and he lived it more than any of us will ever know. He knew the great quest. Matt Feeney equals the same kind of warrior. He lives and he enters the 'ring' each day.

For, you see, like Teddy Roosevelt said, "It is not the critic who counts: not the man who points out how the strong man stumbles or where the doer of deeds could have done better. The credit belongs to the man who is actually in the arena, whose face is marred by dust and sweat and blood, who strives valiantly, who errs and comes up short again and again, because there is no effort without error or shortcoming, but who knows the great enthusiasms, the great devotions, who spends himself for a worthy cause; who, at the best, knows, in the end, the triumph of high achievement, and who, at the worst, if he fails, at least he fails while daring greatly, so that his place shall never be with those cold and timid souls who knew neither victory nor defeat." "Citizenship in a Republic," Speech at the Sorbonne, Paris, April 23, 1910.

I don't know how they do it. But the fact is, they live it. If they can do it, they inspire us to do it at whatever level we might want to try our quest. That's where legends like Steve Mulholland and Matt Feeney take us by their actions.

That's why Lava Falls thrills die-hard rafters. It's their moment of glory or death.

I used the Groover early before anyone got up. Using it is a remarkable aspect of a raft trip because it provides an ethereal experience. You don't stare at a wall and roll of toilet paper. It's not the same old thing each morning. No, using the Groover is a moment of contemplative quiet with the eternal ongoing mystery of the Grand Canyon and the Colorado River quietly painting majestic scenes before you as you enjoy your morning constitutional. It's never the same and it's always amazing. There! One big mark AGAINST a five star hotel! Yippee ki yo ki yea!

Later, Strat and I got into a conversation by the river. He talked about his job as a wood craftsman—about struggling for money but his life was his own.

"No stress from above, or below," he said referring to no boss or employees.

Hollywood (my friend Gary) walked up.

"Hollywood had the same thing, but then he got married," Strat said with a sly smile.

"Yeah, I was newly retired and said to myself…hum, no more stress from the top, none from the bottom… guess I'll get married," Gary mused.

We laughed.

Brenda called out for breakfast.

Wocnis walked up to Badger with a cut in his left index finger. He had nearly sliced it off. Rick would have to row Lava Falls.

"I'll pray for both of you," Steve said.

We felt terrible that Wocnis cut himself so badly that he couldn't oar the boat. But secretly, I knew Rick yearned to row that rapid. He would get to captain the biggest, scariest rapid on the river. He showed his eagerness, too, like a true adventurer. He wanted to try the unknown. He purposely got out there on the edge the cliff to peer over and crawl back, to see what was there—to discover not only the treasure—but to discover himself—test himself—enjoy himself. It's what took him to the top of Mount Rainier, Kilimanjaro and the tests he faced on the Zambezi. To top it off, he flames into life with a heck of a lot of laughter. Not even being a dish fairy could stop his tenacity in the face of deadly danger. He became a true river rat. His mother would be proud.

Wendell Barry said, "And the world cannot be discovered by a journey of miles, no matter how long, but only by a spiritual journey, a journey of one inch, very arduous and humbling and joyful, by which we arrive at the ground at our feet, and learn to be at home."

On August 25, 1869, Powell wrote: "Great quantities of lava are seen on either side; and then we come to an abrupt. Just over the fall a cinder cone, or extinct volcano stands on the very brink of the canyon. What a conflict of water and fire there must have been here! Just imagine a river of molten rock running down into a river of melted snow. What a seething and boiling of the waters; what clouds of steam rolled into the heavens!"

In the late morning, we reached Lava Falls at mile marker 179. Everyone tied up 'river right' and hiked to the rapid. My God! We witnessed an unholy, raging, and terrifying stretch of 900 feet of pure seething white water fury. We could hardly hear one another's voices.

I ran down through the rocks to take up a photo point near the huge hole at the end of the tongue. A thousand caged and angry lions could not have competed with the deafening roar of white water. Exhilaration coursed through my body. THIS excited every cell in my body! If you can tap into this stuff, death is a definite possibility.

One by one, everyone returned to their rafts and prepared themselves.

Badger and Steve rowed into the holocaust first. Steve hollered as Badger worked the oars. They hit the first hole and the boat shot skyward. Steve looked like a hood ornament on a 57 Pontiac.

I snapped a picture. Nothing but a water white-out and their raft crashing through it! OUTRAGEOUS!

They careened into the next hole and slid by Cheese Grater Rock. It's called that because if you didn't pull away from it fast enough, you would become instantly grated like cheese! Moments later, they dropped into the calmness of an eddy.

Next, Ivan and Brenda slid down the maw of the green glassy tongue of the devil. They got caught in some laterals, which pushed Brenda to work the front of the boat. At the hole, Ivan's raft plowed through the pillow at the top, but as he did, the boat slid to the right. The seething froth sucked him further to the right and he headed straight into Cheese Grater Rock. He hit it, too, dead on. Ivan reefed on the oars, but the slant of the water nearly tossed him out of the boat. Brenda stepped to the high side to keep the boat from flipping.

Ivan gained the oars and powered them enough to pull the boat back into the rapids. Seconds later, they escaped.

Everyone cheered!

SCARY! Even MORE thrilling!

I jumped up with adrenaline shooting through my body. I ran back to where Gary had streamlined his raft. He stashed all gear including the ammo boxes. I folded and secured the chairs. We cinched our helmets.

Where Hance Rapid scared me more than excited me, Lava excited and SCARED me to a fever pitch. If we lived, we lived! And, if we died, well, we died! What the hell!

"Let's do it," I said to Gary.

We drifted out behind Rick and Wocnis.

Behind us, Sally and Strat eased into the river. I detected a mischievous look on Sally's face—as if she dared the river to give her a wild ride—and that she would come out on top. She resembled the look of an 18-year old girl's excitement encased in the wisdom of a woman of the world.

"Have a great run," Strat said.

"You the same," Gary said.

In the blink of an eye, Captain Rick positioned his boat near the big rock, swept past it into the left lateral and missed the big hole. He rowed with intelligence, but the kid in him screamed with pleasure. The boat, with Wocnis in front and holding his throbbing finger in the air, smashed through the waves, but headed too far to the right, and again into Cheese Grater Rock—to seemingly be devoured and turned into taco condiment. But, at the last second, Rick pulled hard on the oars to bring the boat off to the left, but not enough to stop it from kissing the Grater Rock. Whereby, Wocnis, in a moment of white water delirium, stuck his hand out and touched Cheese Grater Rock in defiance.

The last we saw them, the boat fell over a huge wall of white and vanished down river.

"Rick made it!" I yelled back at Gary as we too swept into the green stillness of the Lava Falls tongue.

Black lava comes up from hell and from the roar before us, it felt like we were being swallowed back into the Devil's kingdom. But the kingdom was not fire and heat—but an aspirin white swirling tornado of screaming froth—boiling angry—mad as hell—nature at its best.

Into it we plunged!

Gary eased us into the middle and swung the 'River Slug' into the first hole. I held on to both straps and pressed my feet onto the front air bladder of the raft.

Down, down, down until we crashed into the dead end at the bottom of the hole. The front end buckled my knees back at me like Sear's best Monroe-Matic shock absorbers. The 'Slug' regained itself and began the climb out of hell.

I held my breath.

At the top of the skyscraper of water, the river gods decided to throw a 40-gallon bucket of water into my face. I recoiled into the raft seat and clung to my straps. It felt like I was on the Andrea Dorea in "The Perfect Storm."

Icy cold! Cruel! Refreshing like a Coors commercial!

"YEEEEEHAAAAAA," I screamed. "Give 'em hell Gary!"

We crashed through a world of roaring, screaming white water rage—swirling in every direction and carrying us toward Cheese Grater Rock. Gary stood on the oars until he got us out away from the rock, but into three more skyscraper waves.

We smashed into them like a demolition derby and still came out the other side in one piece. I pulled the bucket out as 12 inches of water surrounded my feet.

"I'm bailing," I yelled. "Great job Gary! You ARE the MAN!"

Strat and Sally followed us into that wild mouse ride. I saw Sally ride the front end of the 'cat' and she too, took that wall of white water and busted into it like Annie Oakley doing trick-shooting from her horse.

There wasn't a dry inch of skin on her body, but there was a Grand Canyon wide smile on her face.

We put in on a sandbar to celebrate with salmon, crackers, artichoke hearts, beer, cookies and M&Ms for lunch. Lava Falls turned out to be a rite of passage—a portal into the 'club' of river runners.

Everyone applauded each other's moment.

For me, I had faced my fear. Maybe not like Powell and his men faced fear—for theirs was a journey truly into the unknown. In fact, three of them left the adventure BECAUSE of their fears. Incidentally, Indians killed them when they hiked out of the canyon.

But this was the 21st century, and in my own way for my time, I looked the monster in the face and decided to go for it. I think every person in this life, at least those of us fortunate enough not to be starving to death in a country or culture that suffocates the human spirit—moves forward on an evolutionary trek. None of us know what's going to happen tomorrow. Excitingly enough, tomorrow is not guaranteed to anyone. As Helen Keller said, "Life is either a daring adventure or nothing. Security is mostly a superstition. It does not exist in nature." Thus, we move into the future with a sense of adventure because that is our nature.

Lava Falls still roars like a thousand lions this very minute. Day after day, century after century, through the ages. For a moment in time, I ran that rapid, and didn't die. I lived and the THRILL of it will remain with me for my lifetime.

CHAPTER 14—Tales of Highwater Harry

> *"In God's wildness lies the hope of the world—the great, fresh, unblighted, unredeemed wilderness. The galling harness of civilization drops off, and the wounds heal ere we are aware."*
> John Muir

We camped at a hundred-yard-long by forty-yard-wide sandbar. The sand looked Cancun white and felt soft under our feet. Badger planted his Bugs Bunny flag and Hollywood brought out his chipping wedge with 20 golf balls. Next, they drove stakes and a lively game of horseshoes commenced. They said that Doug Egelston was the top horseshoe thrower on previous raft trips, but in his absence, Hollywood kicked everybody's butts. The women grabbed a big rubber float and paddled around in tandem. Wocnis broke out three Frisbees.

Strat, Ivan, Steve and I got into a bull session.

Later, the women cooked dinner.

As usual, three dish fairies swooped in after supper and cleaned up the whole place after the typical feast. Of course, they complained as usual.

"Soap suds on my wings make it hard for me to fly," Fairy Steve said.

"I broke a nail," Fairy Rick said.

"My fairy dust got soaked when you threw that wet dish towel at me," Fairy Frosty said.

"Quit complaining and GET those dishes done," Brenda ordered.

Later, I walked out to a large boulder on the point. One of the things I noticed in two weeks on the river was the loss of a sense of time. Day or night! No schedule. I enjoyed a more profound connection to the earth. I walked in bare feet most of the time and the sand squeezed between my toes and the waters soaked my feet. The bushes and rocks scratched me when I hiked in the canyons. I watched my foot-fall each time. I felt the cool of the river and the heat of the sun. I sun-burned my ankles. In the canyon wilderness, nothing artificial existed. There hadn't been a trace of civilization for 14 days. No cars, radio, highways, bridges or roads. I lived out in the middle of nature and nature lived deep inside of me.

Out of nowhere, I heard a rock crash into the water. Looking up, I watched Sally throwing big rocks over the edge of a cliff some 50 feet above the river. She had thrown rocks more than once on this journey. Made me wonder if she threw away the past and moved into the future? During the trip, we had celebrated Cindy's 50th birthday.

Although some might malign their advancing age, I find it a joy JUST to still be here. We toasted our friend Doug's return to health from his battles with cancer. Badger's heart attack sobered him. As I looked around the camp, I saw 11 human beings sharing the wilderness with me. Each of them engaged separate struggles—whether it be health, money, marriage, emotional or spiritual. None of us gets out of this life without a great number of bumps and bruises brought on by life's lessons.

In the morning, I walked back out to that rock. I am sitting on it while writing this adventure story.

I watch the emerald green water roll by. It runs swift and garnished with white water music. Above me, fluffy cotton candy clouds slowly turn from pink to silver and white. The canyon walls light up in red and tan. High rock cathedral spires stretch toward the limitless azure sky. A Blue Heron glides past me on his breakfast patrol. His wings turn brilliant blue when he flies into the sunshine. The last bat makes one more snack run and heads for his hideout before the sun catches him and he becomes a meal for a hawk. Out here, someone always feeds on someone else.

Sitting on this rock, I am trying to think of something but realize in the past two weeks that I have lost all thoughts, all worries, all concerns, and all problems. My life and everyone's on this journey anchors in the present. We enjoy astonishing scenery, laughter from Rick's jokes, horseshoes, food, wildlife sprinkled through the day and night like sugar and cinnamon on toast—and, added to it, spiritual bliss.

By mid-morning, we eased out into the river at mile marker 210. There we sat, five rafts and 12 people. Rapid after rapid greeted us with white water fury. Sandstone cliff walls rose up from the river. Canyons broke into our canyon and multiple black lava flows dropped into the Colorado, but were frozen in time. We viewed seven separate volcanic eruptions from the past. They looked like someone had poured black cake batter from the heavens and it oozed through the red sandstone corridors to freeze into place like dark chocolate crystal icing. Some of the lava flows hit the bottom and suffered erosion by the water—leaving them looking like endless miles of draperies like the ones they lower at the movies and pull them back up before the show.

By mid morning, we passed a huge cave in the red rock 2,000 feet above us.

"Wonder how that cave got cut out?" I said. "Must be big enough to put a 747 jetliner inside."

"Maybe two," Gary said.

"This place never ceases to amaze me each day," I said.

We stopped for lunch on a sandbar. For some unknown reason, Gary stood around with a shit-eating grin on his face. He didn't say anything. He didn't have to.

I sang, "I feel good and I knew that I would now."

"You know," Badger said. "Someone always sings that James Brown song on every trip about this time."

Cindy and Sally had been rowing their boats, which made them hungry. Brenda broke out the food. We ate some moldy old bread but no one complained. We cut off the mold. Sandwiches never tasted so good.

Rick shared a few funnies and we laughed. Steve talked about the history of WW II and how it affected us today. Strat talked about the futility and intrigue of politics. Ivan talked about his Alpaca farm. Wocnis presented us with a picture of the "GRAND CANYON DISH FAIRIES." We all smiled.

Everyone's personality had flourished on the trip via what he or she said and who they were as a person. Each of us humans proves a one-time rendition in the whole of the universe—never to be repeated. But none of it mattered down here in this ancient geological masterpiece. We became friends sharing an amazing adventure in the Grand Canyon.

That night after dinner, I recited the "Cremation of Sam McGee" by Robert Service. It was a cold dog sledding tale from the far north in the Yukon. Rick sang a song about "Them Bones." Strat played guitar while singing a number of songs he had written. Wocnis added his talents on the harmonica. Our voices carried into the night air.

As we sat around in a circle, Wocnis, grizzled with beard and scraggly hair, stepped into the gathering like some mystic in the night. He began a tale about the exploits of the devil and a man whom might best him on an outlaw run down the Grand Canyon. Wocnis sat down in the campfire circle, wiped the foam off his mouth from the beer he drank and recited his "Ballad of Highwater Harry":

> "Now listen well this tale I tell,
> 'bout a river mean and cruel;
> And Highwater Harry, a rafting pal,
> As brave as any fool.
>
> A giant flood of water and mud,
> Had raced across the land...
> And swollen streams with bursting seams,
> All joined the river Grand. (earlier name for the Colorado River)
>
> Now Harry was a river rat,
> Who'd float most anything;
> He said he knew a favorite run,
> To liven-up the spring!
>
> We drove down to the river,
> Where a ranger waited there;

Rafting the Rolling Thunder

And my knees began to quiver,
As he made his warning clear.

The ranger said "No boatin'...
Cause the water, it's too high;
If I let you all afloatin'
You'd surely all would die!"

But Harry said we'd come too far,
As we drove back up the road;
In a secret spot he parked the car,
And started to unload.

We rigged the raft from fore to aft,
And hid just out of sight...
And while the ranger was a sleepin'
We'd drift by in the night!

Hours passed and then at last,
The moon commenced to shine;
I got aboard and grabbed the oars,
While Harry held the line.

He said to me, "You'll love this float!"
As he grinned from ear to ear;
But me, I felt this midnight trip,
Was dangerous and pretty queer!

But Harry said we're ready,
It's time that we embark;
Then we turned around at a rustlin' sound,
As a stranger crept from the dark!

"I've never seen it bigger,"
The stranger flatly said.
"There ain't no one can float it,
'Cept the fools and the dead!"

Now Harry is a brazen sport,
A braggart through and through...

He gave that old man quite the snort,
And said what he could do:

"There ain't no river I can't ride,
No rapids got me yet...
I can float the likes o' this,
And never once get wet!"

"And furthermore, I've seen holes galore,
And waves up to the sky...
I bet my life, my kids and wife,
This river I can ride!"

The stranger spat and grinned a bit,
Said, "Son, you've got yourself a bet;
In fact, I think I'll go along,
Just to see whar' you get 'et!"

Then Harry scoffed in a voice so low,
"By God, we'll let this old man go!
He's earned a chance to see firsthand,
How Harry rides the River Grand!"

But I was taken some aback,
By this stranger who was dressed in black;
Who found us here in the dull moonlight,
With eyes that glowed when seen just right.

But it's Harry's trip, so I held my peace,
And the river helped my mind to cease;
Thinkin' 'bout this strange old man,
Who came along just to see us damned!

We drifted high and easy,
This river swift but calm...
I was startin' to feel queasy,
'Bout the canyon just beyond.

The water was cold and muddy,
And many fathoms deep;

Rafting the Rolling Thunder

It boiled in raging madness,
Through the gorges cramped and steep.

The walls rose high and jagged,
And the river, it was squeezed;
The waves got tall and ragged,
As the water picked up speed.

Our raft did twist and buck and dive,
Thru waves of frothing white...
I wondered yet 'bout Harry's bet,
With the stranger in the night!

We paddled on toward the dawn,
Through the rapids' awful roar...
Crashing walls, down waterfalls,
Each rapid threatening more.

Several times through river's maw,
Whilst the stranger bent to bail;
'neath his cloak I thought I saw,
A thin and pointed tail.

Next, there came a wave so big,
It snapped our oars like tiny twigs!
Like limpets clung against the surf,
We held on tight for all we're worth!

Each rapid bigger than the last,
My strength and courage waving fast...
The stranger turned, he laughed and said:
"Big Daddy Rapid up ahead!"

Harry's strength had stayed him good,
As Harry always bragged it would;
He said no wave could flip his raft...
Big rocks and holes just made him laugh!

Then the canyon narrowed more,
And up ahead an awesome roar...

The walls were straight and sharp as glass,
'Big Daddy Rapid' comin' FAST!

Then panic struck my desperate mood,
I grabbed and yanked that stranger's hood;
And tearing off his thin disguise,
Revealed his horns and devilish eyes!

The moments then were all as one,
As down the tongue our raft was flung;
Then swallowed 'neath a massive boil,
To flounder lost in the river's toil!

The raft was crushed and ripped apart,
And all was thrown asunder...
I prayed to God with all my heart,
As the current pulled us under.

After that, it all went black,
How long, I cannot say...
I awoke at last with choking gasps,
To beach sand where I lay.

The devil lay there next to me,
His face into the ground...
And even I could plainly see,
That Satan had been drowned!

Now Harry stood there grinning
And said, "About that bet....
I had to choke that devil,
"Cause I sure as hell got wet!"

After that brush with death, Wocnis, with a glint in his eye, stood up in the night shadows. He turned and walked down to the river's edge. In moments, he crept onto his raft and found his bed. As quick as a shooting star, he curled into his sleeping bag while staring up at the ink black of eternity.

If I didn't know any better, I would bet he began scheming his next outlaw run, with the slight of his hand, down "the River Grand."

CHAPTER 15—How fast our lives sweep past

> *"It rains! Rapidly little rills formed above, and these soon grew into brooks, and the brooks grew into creeks and tumble over the walls in innumerable cascades, adding their wild music to the roar of the river. The waters that fall during a rain on these steep rocks are gathered at once into the river; they could scarcely be poured in more suddenly as if some vast spout ran from the clouds to the stream itself."*
>
> Major John Wesley Powell
> 1869

It rained today while we floated on still waters. We rafted over a few small rapids, which gave us time for quiet reflection. When the sky broke gray in the mid afternoon, the temperature plummeted to 70 degrees. The first rain drops sprinkled us, but soon, the sky opened up and drenched the landscape. It wasn't a harsh, wind-driven rain, but a serene one. The drops plunked on the water creating a silvery sheen of mist. Each raft in front of us looked like a colorful toy winging through the gray mist that looked like a ground level fog from dry ice. The rhythmic swing of each set of oars created movement as they dropped into the water and rose again. I watched a dream unfold in the mist ahead of me.

Rafting the Rolling Thunder

Yesterday, we had stopped at Pumpkin Springs: a boiling spring that had formed into a pumpkin from travertine deposits being built up over time. We ate lunch and enjoyed the scenery. Everyone started talking about life back in the big city.

Our camp on the last night at mile marker 220 had been like an Oasis Island with trees and beach leading down to the river. As usual, the guys started a bull session on Badger's boat. On an earlier expedition, they had nearly run up on Lava Falls before scouting it—and joked about their near disaster from that mistake. You could laugh if you lived through it.

Soon, Brenda, Cindy and Sally walked over with crackers, cheese, beers and snacks.

Laughter prevailed.

Up river, the last rapid we had run rendered a muffled roar.

At that moment, we rafted only four miles to the Diamond Creek take-out. I looked back at Gary as he oared away with happy abandoned. Our 16-day run rushed toward an ending.

It's amazing how fast our lives sweep past. Whether I've been on the front end of a ten-month 8,000-mile bicycle ride across an entire continent or a two-day ski trip—it always comes to an end. Just like John Wesley Powell's! He wrote in his time. It was alive and real for him at that moment. Now he is dead. His moment passed. I am still here and all those who share it with me on this trip.

At this moment I am thankful for being fortunate enough to have been able to go in the first place. Like

John Muir, I will always stand in nature with a sense of wonder, awe and gratitude.

Before the take-out, one last rapid awaited and did not disappoint. I hooted and hollered with water soaking me as usual. Gary smiled.

Up ahead, Diamond Creek Mountain struck a sharp triangular point into the sky.

Before we knew it, a flurry of activity on 'river left' took place with rafts being inflated and people running about the landing. Our transport truck awaited us on the gray rocky gravel. A dusty road that cut up through a canyon provided the only way out and led to Peach Springs, Arizona where we could pick up our cars that had been driven by a transport agency.

We hit the beach and began breaking down the rafts. A man in a truck backed up and helped us put all our gear in place. For one last moment, the 12 of us got a group photograph along the river. Moments later, we boarded a bus on our way to pick up our cars and head home.

As I sat by the window on the bus, my mind raced back to that first moment of meeting everyone at Lee's Ferry. At that time, I remained clueless. Just another raft trip! A river was a river. What was the big deal?

The BIG deal, as I found out, this river cuts through one of the most phenomenal geological masterpieces that this galaxy has ever created.

There are few 'last' frontiers on our crowded little planet—Antarctica, the Mato Grosso Jungle of Brazil, the Congo, parts of Siberia, the Galapagos Islands, the Great Barrier Reef, the Outback of Australia and this vast, timeless, majestic canyon that stretches across time. I'm glad I rafted this one. I'm glad Hance Rapid terrified me. I thrilled to the power of Horned Creek and Upset Rapid. And, I met my fears by running Lava Falls. The heat, sand, scorpions, mice, bats and butterflies—all were a part of nature's gifts to every one of us. Yes, we'll run more rivers and climb more mountains. Indeed, life sweeps past much like a river and we humans manifest an ephemeral blink on the landscape. Nonetheless, I'm thankful to the universe for my moment in this ancient canyon of time.

Henry David Thoreau said, "If you advance confidently in the direction of your dreams, and endeavor to live the life which you have imagined, you will meet with success unexpected in common hours. You will pass through an invisible boundary; new universal and liberal laws will begin to establish themselves; and you will live with a license of a higher order of beings."

I'll count this adventure as one of the twenty best in my lifetime. And, although it is over—it remains in my eyes, mind and spirit for the rest of my life.

The End

CHAPTER 16—River friends and last Powell report

> *"If you're alive, you need to flap your wings and make some noise—let people know you exist. Because life is the very opposite of death."*
> Mel Brooks

The following characters made the Grand Canyon adventure shared moments of friendship. Each contributed in his or her own way. By Canyon Sally.

They are as follows:

BLAZING BRENDA Celtic river conqueror Slayer of streams, leader of teams Taming the turbulence of details by the reams

INVINCIBLE IVAN Always on the row A smoke for the slow go Quietly confident, he goes with the flow

CINNAMON CINDY Steady and ready like red canyon walls Knows when to hold 'em, knows when to walk 'em, And knows when to swim

RANGER SCOUT RICK Runs the big one Sings the silly ones, puns on anyone Sweet seeker of fun

Rafting the Rolling Thunder

GRACEFUL GARY Gliding and guiding his raft on and on down the river Pie after pie after brownie Dancing in his mind

JOYFUL JULIE Elegant energy, beautifully bubbling Eyes always sparkling Discovering delights

FIESTY FROSTY A fiery fountain of thoughts and feelings unfolding Filling pages and people with floods of facts, Waves of conviction and cresting quotes of note

STEADY STEVE A man with a story and muscles of glory Facing wave after wave, dish after spoon Ready to help, morning till moon

BENVEOLENT BADGER Bearing bits of river wisdom Warns of rapids and rocks, knows of camps and creeks, Silently seeking secreted sweets

WANDERING WOCNIS Tracker of trails, tossed parasols And lines of lively language Impish innocent eyes animate and a Wocian world of wonders

STRAPPIN' STRAT Serenading our souls, creating new rhymes:
"Bilge, bags, straps and ties, what does it take to kill some flies?"

CANYON SALLY Thinker and feeler way out on a rock, Of her mental meanderings there is no block, Sensual wondering—her eyes on the human race, A woman with passion and loving grace.

"Time is a companion that goes with us on a journey. It reminds us to cherish each moment, because it will never come again. What we leave behind is not as important as how we lived." Captain Jean Luc Picard, Starship Enterprise.

August 29, 1869—"The relief from danger and the joy of success are great. When he who has been chained by wounds to a hospital cot…at last goes out into the open field, what a world he sees! The first hour of convalescent freedom seems rich recompense for all the pain, gloom and terror. Something like these are the feelings we experience tonight…the river rolls by us in silent majesty; the quiet of the camp is sweet; our joy is almost ecstasy."

> John Wesley Powell
> Last day on the river

About the Author

Frosty Wooldridge graduated from Michigan State University. He is an environmentalist, mountain climber, Scuba diver, dancer, skier, writer, speaker and photographer. He has taught at the elementary, high school and college levels. He bicycled 100,000 miles on six continents and six times across the United States. His feature articles have appeared in national and international magazines for 30 years. He has interviewed on NBC, CBS, ABC, CNN, FOX and 150 radio shows. He writes bi-weekly columns for 40 web sites including www.freedomsphoenix.com ; www.NewsWithViews.com ; www.AmericanChronicle.com; www.neighbors.DenverPost.com ; www.beforeitsnews.com His books include:

Handbook for Touring Bicyclists--Bicycling touring is growing in popularity each year. Men and women around the world are taking to the highways and the "open air" is their kitchen. On the pages of this book, you'll discover how to buy, carry, prepare, and store food while on tour. Discover the 'ins and outs' with a "Bakers Dozen" of touring tips that are essential for successful bicycle adventuring. Whether you're going on a weekend ride, a week-long tour, or two years around the world, this handbook will help you learn the artistry of bicycling and cooking.

Strike Three! Take Your Base--The Brookfield Reader, Sterling, VA; 2001. ISBN 1-930093-01-2. To order this hardcover book, send $19.95 to Frosty Wooldridge, POB 207, Louisville, CO 80027. This poignant story is important reading for every teen that has ever experienced the loss of a parent from either death or divorce. This is the story of a boy losing his father and growing through his sense of pain and loss. It is the story of baseball - a game that was shared by both the boy and his father - and how baseball is much like life.

An Extreme Encounter: Antarctica—"This book transports readers into the bowels of million year old glaciers, katabatic winds, to the tops of smoking volcanoes, scuba diving under the ice, wacky people, death, outlaw activities and rare moments where he meets penguins, whales, seals and Skua birds. Hang on to your seat belts--you're in for a wild ride where the bolt goes into the bottom of the world." Sandy Colhoun, editor-in-chief, The Antarctic Sun.

Bicycling Around the World: Tire Tracks for your Imagination--This book mesmerizes readers with animal stories that bring a smile to your face. It will pain your mind and heart seeing the Third World. It chills you with a once-in-a-lifetime ride in Antarctica where you'll meet a family of Emperor penguins. Along the way, you'll find out that you have to go without a mirror, sometimes, in order to see yourself. The greatest aspect of this book comes from--expectation! Not since 'Miles from Nowhere' has a writer captured the Zen and Art of Bicycle Adventure as well as Wooldridge. Not only that, you enjoy a final section-'EVERYTHING YOU NEED TO KNOW ABOUT LONG DISTANCE TOURING'. He shows you 'HOW TO LIVE THE DREAM'. You'll have the right bike, equipment, money and tools to ride into your own long distance touring adventures. If you like bicycling, you'll go wild reading this book. If you don't like bicycling, you'll still go wild reading this book.

Motorcycle Adventure to Alaska: Into the Wind—"Seldom does a book capture the fantasy and reality of an epic journey the magnitude of a 'MOTORCYCLE ADVENTURE TO ALASKA'. Trevor and Dan resemble another duo rich in America's history of youthful explorers who get into all kinds of trouble - Tom Sawyer and Huckleberry Finn. They plied the Mississippi River, but Dan and his brother push their machines into a wild and savage land—Alaska. My boys loved it." John Mathews, father of two boys and a daughter.

Bicycling the Continental Divide: Slice of Heaven, Taste of Hell—"This bicycle dream ride carries a bit of Tom Sawyer and Huckleberry Finn. The author mixes hope with adventure, pain with courage and bicycling with mountains. John Brown, a friend left behind to battle cancer, provides guts and heart for his two friends who ride into the teeth of nature's fury. Along the way, you'll laugh, cry and gain new appreciations while pondering the meaning of life."

Immigration's Unarmed Invasion: Deadly Consequences—"Few challenges throughout history will affect the course of human events like the topic of this book. Immigration, both legal and illegal, will determine if America is to survive as a viable, prosperous nation into the 21st Century or sink into the depths of poverty. Wooldridge offers a thorough examination of this topic with exhaustive research and critical thinking." - *Kenneth R. Hampshire, President, Advanced Health Group.*

America on the Brink: The Next Added 100 Million Americans—"Electrifying reading! This is a veritable cannonade of a book. Wooldridge targets the people and institutions, from the President on down, who refuse to look at the consequences of population growth in the modern era. His focus is on the United States, but his range is the world. He fearlessly addresses issues that politicians fear to mention, such as the effects of mass immigration on our population future and our social systems. He engages to force population issues into our local and national political decisions." - *Lindsey Grant, former Deputy Assistant Secretary of State for Environment and Population.*

Losing Your Best Friend: Vacancies of the Heart— "This is one heck of a powerful book! It's a must read for anyone that has lost a friend or parent. It will give you answers that you may not have thought about. It will touch your heart and you will learn from their experiences. It also shows you what you can do if you suffer conflict with your friend's wife or girlfriend." Jonathan Runy.

Misty's Long Ride: Across America on Horseback— *Misty's Long Ride*, by Smooth Georgia Mist (Howard Wooldridge - Frosty Wooldridge's brother), AuthorHouse, 2005. ISBN 1-4208-5766-5 (sc). "As good as Howard was, sometimes there was nothing he could do about our situation in the burning inferno of Utah. In that agonizing desert, a man's mouth became so dry, he couldn't spit. I felt the heat cook my hooves at ground level where it felt like walking alone in the middle of a farrier's furnace. Above us, vultures soared in the skies searching for road-kill. Yet, Howard pulled down the brim of his hat and pushed forward. I followed this cowboy because he was a Long Rider and I was his horse...." For anyone who loves horses and high adventure - Howard's horse Misty tells one of the great adventure tales in the 21st century by galloping coast to coast across America. You'll enjoy horse sense, horse humor, unique characters and ride the wild wind.

All books available at: 1 888 280 7715, www.amazon.com , www.barnesandnoble.com Wooldridge presents a program to conferences and colleges across the USA: *"The Coming Population Crisis in America: and what you can do about it."* He lives in Louisville, CO www.frostywooldridge.com

Made in the USA
Lexington, KY
18 March 2011